Reignite and Reinvent Your Marriage

A Companion to The Marriage Journey

Chuck and Mae Dettman

Copyright © 2022

Chuck and Mae Dettman All rights reserved.

ISBN-10: 0-9972338-1-8
ISBN-13: 978-0-9972338-1-0

This publication is intended to provide accurate information regarding the subject matter covered. It is sold with the understanding that neither the authors nor the publisher are engaged in rendering psychological, financial or other professional services. If professional assistance or counseling is needed, the services of a competent professional should be sought.

Referencing of materials in this book is not meant to imply any endorsement of the author, publisher, or organization that created those materials.

Copyright © 2018 Chuck and Mae Dettman. All rights reserved.

All rights reserved. No part of this publication may be reproduced, stored in a retrieval system, or transmitted in any form or by any means— electronic, mechanical, photocopying, recording, or otherwise— without the prior written permission of the authors. The only exception is brief quotations in printed reviews.

Unless otherwise noted, all scripture verses used are from THE HOLY BIBLE, NEW INTERNATIONAL VERSION®, NIV® Copyright ©

1973, 1978, 1984, 2010 by Biblica, Inc. ™ Used by permission. All rights reserved worldwide.

All images are used under Creative Commons CC0 licensure unless otherwise attributed in the image.

1. Marriage-Religious aspects-Christianity. 2. Marriage-Biblical teaching. 3. Relationships. 4. Interpersonal relations–Religious aspects–Christianity. 5. Conflict management-Religious aspects-Christianity.

This book is available in large quantity discounts for use in denominational or regional marriage initiatives and can be customized with your organization or denomination's logo. For more information, contact **ChuckD@TheMarriage- Journey.com.**

Printed in the United States of America.

Introduction

Have you ever considered rating your marriage? On a 1-10 scale where do you think your marriage rates? Do you often wonder if there is more, if it could get better?

What about sharing a gift of growth in your relationship? Strengthen your love, grow your heart and become the husband and wife many will envy.

We give attention to almost every element of our surroundings (vehicles, homes, clothing, offices, body, and more), but neglect our marriages. Consider this: if you never change the oil in the vehicle, what happens? It breaks down and stops running. Neglect the home and it also becomes uninhabitable over time. Fitness Centers, Diet Programs, and Pharmaceuticals bombard us with advertisements to support healthy lifestyles; all attempting to convince us we 'need their product to maintain health.' Do you ever see the same philosophy applied to our marriages? Left without maintenance, they too will become unhealthy. Not once have we seen an advertisement directed toward building a healthy, strong and lasting marriage on the evening news, during Prime Time TV or as a sponsor for a major sports event! Why? Most likely because we take marriage for granted— and no one has figured out how to profit from healthy marriages. There is more money to be made in divorces. Lawyers, accountants and auctioneers benefit from divorces. Nobody makes a dime if you are blissfully married.

Don't wait until you reach a "crumbling" hurdle! Every couple, regardless of how long they've been married, will experience events that can destroy the relationship. Think not *if*, *but when* you'll face job loss, death of a parent, child or pet, anniversary of a traumatic experience. All left untouched without the tools knowing how to navigate the opportunity your marriage could implode. **Learn today, to strengthen tomorrow!**

Reignite and Reinvent Your Marriage is designed to provide faith-based skills and habits that will build and strengthen your marriage. ***Reignite and Reinvent*** is a safe place for you and your spouse to reconnect; whether you rate your relationship as a 1 or 10, or anywhere in between. The principles shared in this companion are *'a process'* and not magical. Give yourself fully to the gift of the process and watch how God changes you, your marriage and family.

Know that your leaders are praying for you and look forward to what God has in store for you and your spouse in the weeks to come.

Table of Contents

Introduction 3

Chapter 1 13

Our Union With Christ 13

God Is The Pilot; We Are the Co-pilots 13

LearningObjectives 13

Introduction 13

Why is this topic important? 14

What Does the Bible Say? 14

Common Concerns Regarding Union with Christ 15

Navigational Aids 15

In-Flight Checklist 16

Chapter 2 17

The Biblical Roles of Husbands and Wives 17

Learning Objectives 17

Introduction 17

Why is this topic important? 18

What Does the Bible Say? 19

Types of Roles 20

Primary Roles 21

The Meaning of Marriage 21

His Primary Roles & Responsibilities 23

Her Primary Roles & Responsibilities 25

Shared Roes of Husbands & Wives 26

Secondary Roles 27

Principles Related to Roles 27

Issues Regarding Roles in Marriage 28

What other sources of influence have impacted you or others you know? 28

Navigation Aids 28

In-Flight Checklist 28

Chapter 3 30

Communicating 30

The Control Tower is Calling 30

LearningObjectives 30

Introduction 31

Why is this topic important? 31

What Does the Bible Say? 32

Common Concerns Regarding Communicating 33

Discussion Starters 33

Identifying a Couple's Primary 34

Communication Style 34

Identifying & Interpreting the Results 35

Four Common Communication Styles 36

How Did Jesus Communicate? 37

What about Passive-Aggressive? 37

The Impact on Intimacy 38

How Threats & Anxiety Drive Our Response 38

How to be More Assertive 39

Don't be Overly Assertive 39

If you over use assertiveness 39

Active Listening 40

Practice the Three Steps to Better Communication 40

Chapter 4 .... *41*

Conflict Resolution – Navigating Turbulence 41

Learning Objectives 41

Introduction 41

Why is this topic important? 42

What Does the Bible Say? 42

Discussion Starters 43

Common Issues Regarding Conflict Resolution 43

"The Problem" Isn't the Real Problem 44

Resolving Conflict has Two Components 44

Resolving Conflict Well 45

10-Steps to Resolving Conflict 46

Conflict Resolution Style 47

Emotional Intensity & Disagreement Style 48

- Constructive & Destructive Approaches to Conflict Resolution 49
- When Couples Need Outside Help 49

Chapter 5 .... *50*

- Granting Forgiveness - Let God Navigate 50
- Your Heart 50
- Learning Objectives 50
- Introduction 50
- Why is this topic important? 51
- What Does the Bible Say? 51
- Forgiveness Myths 52
- True Forgiveness 52
- Forgiveness Is Not 53
- Forgiveness Is 53
- Four Promises of Forgiveness 54
- Steps to Forgiveness 54
- Learn To Forgive Yourself 55
- In-Flight Checklist 55
- Referrals 56

Chapter 6 .... *57*

- Trust 57
- The Flight Succeeds with Trust! 57
- Learning Objectives 57
- Introduction 58
- Why is this topic important? 58
- What Does the Bible Say? 59
- 5 Ways to Rebuild Trust 59
- Navigational Aids 60
- In-Flight Checklist 60
- Write Your Story Here 61

Chapter 7 .... *62*

- The Internet, Social Media and Friends - Protecting Your Flight Path 62
- Learning Objectives 62
- Introduction 63
- Why is this topic important? 63
- What Does the Bible Say? 64

Common Concerns Regarding Social Media 64

Tips To Protect Your Marriage Against Social 65

Social Media Items to Consider 66

Social Media Items to Consider 66

Possible Warning Signs 67

Additional Resources 67

Chapter 8 68

Intimacy In Marriage - Enjoy the Flight God's Way 68

LearningObjectives 68

Introduction 68

Why is this topic important? 69

What Does the Bible Say? 70

Common Concerns Regarding Intimacy 70

Four Types of Intimacy In Marriage 71

Navigational Aids 72

In-Flight Checklist 72

Chapter 9 73

Marriage Expectations - The Pre-flight Experience 73

LearningObjectives 73

Introduction 73

Why is this topic important? 74

WhatDoestheBibleSay? 74

Common Concerns Regarding Marriage 75

Expectations 75

Navigational Aids 75

In-Flight Checklist 76

Chapter 10 77

Boundaries 77

Introduction 77

Common Patterns Found in Very Distant Families 78

Common Patterns Found in Very Enmeshed Family Patterns 79

Chapter 11 82

Navigational Cards 82

The Checkpoints Along the Journey 82

Chapter 12 84

- Handling Cultural Differences 84
- Learning Objectives 84
- Introduction 85
- Why is this topic important? 85
- What Does the Bible Say? 86
- Common Concerns Regarding Culturally Different Marriages 86
- Navigational Aids 87
- In-Flight Checklist 88

Chapter 13 89
- Married Again - The 2nd Flight, but Not Together 89
- Learning Objectives 89
- Introduction 89
- Why is this topic important? 90
- What Does the Bible Say? 91
- How To Prepare for Blended Families 92
- NavigationalAids 92
- In-Flight Checklist 93
- Resources 94

Chapter 14 95
- Remarriage 95
- Introduction 95

Chapter 15 98
- Blended Families 98
- Introduction 98

Chapter 16 102
- Becoming Full-Time Caregivers for Your Parent(s) Flying The Historic Airplane 102
- Learning Objectives 102
- Introduction 102
- Why is this topic important? 103
- What Does the Bible Say? 104
- Financial Concerns for Caregivers 104
- You'll take care of me when I'm old...right? 105
- NavigationalAids 105

Chapter 17 106
- Managing and Coping With Stress – 106

- Depart on a Smooth Journey 106
- Learning Objectives 106
- Introduction 106
- Why is this topic important? 107
- What Does the Bible Say? 107
- Common Concerns Regarding Stress 108
- Navigational Aids 109
- In-Flight Checklist 110

Chapter 18 .... *111*
- Managing God's Money 111
- Learning Objectives 111
- Introduction 111
- Why is this topic important? 112
- What Does the Bible Say? 112
- Common Concerns Regarding Finances 113
- 12 Biblical Principles of Wise Financial Management 113
- How Would You Handle These Questions? 114
- Principles of Budgeting 115
- Becoming One Financially 116
- Tips for Merging Finances 116
- Common Money Traps 117
- Aligning Financial Expectations 117
- In-Flight Checklist 118

Chapter 19 .... *119*
- How Cohabitation Impacts the Flight 119
- Learning Objectives 119
- Introduction 119
- What Does the Bible Say? 120
- Common Concerns Regarding Cohabitation 120
- The "Myth" Defused 121
- Adverse Psychological Impact 121
- Couples Over 50 Cohabiting 122
- Cohabitation without Sex 123
- Discussion Starters 123
- In-Flight Checklist 124

Chapter 20 125

   Wedding Day Plans - Planning Your Take-off 125

   Learning Objectives 125

   Introduction 125

   Why is this topic important? 126

   What Does the Bible Say? 126

   Common Concerns Regarding Wedding Planning 127

   Navigation Aides 127

   In-Flight Checklist 128

Chapter 21 129

   The Holidays - Book Your Travel Plans Early 129

   Learning Objectives 129

   Introduction 129

   Why is this topic important? 130

   What Does the Bible Say? 130

   Tips on Holiday Planning 131

   Outsider's Unhealthy Expectations 131

   How to Share Holiday Plans 132

   How to Deal with In-Laws 132

   Shared Custody Planning 133

   List Priorities and Conflicts 133

   Navigation Aides 134

   In-Flight Checklist 135

   Surviving The Holidays: 135

About the Authors 136

Chapter 1
Our Union With Christ
God Is The Pilot; We Are the Co-pilots
Learning Objectives

After this session you will be able to:
- Identify what beliefs are very important to you.
- Are there issues that aren't negotiable?
- What issues are open to compromise?
- How do your beliefs impact how each of you views marriage, roles, priorities, financial decision-making, having children, and parenting?

Introduction

Intimacy in marriage begins with a spiritual relationship with God. The Apostle John writes, *"Dear friends, since God so loved us, we also ought to love one another. No one has ever seen God; but if we love one another, God lives in us and his love is made complete in us."* (1 John 4:11-12)

Developing a strong marriage relationship begins with a commitment to developing a strong relationship with God through Jesus Christ.

Chapter 1

Why is this topic important?

- Spiritual intimacy in marriage is about partnering with God.
- Spiritual intimacy is a decision to walk close to God in obedience, prayer, and meditation on Scripture, fellowship with believers, and service to others. (Acts 2:42)
- Are you willing to make Jesus Christ the Lord of y o u r lives (including your marriage)?

What Does the Bible Say?

_____, *"We have different gifts, according to the grace given us. If a man's gift is prophesying, let him use it in proportion to his faith."*

_____, *"So it is with you. Since you are eager to have spiritual gifts, try to excel in gifts that build up the church."*

_____, *"Do not be yoked together with unbelievers. For what do righteousness and wickedness have in common? Or what fellowship can light have with darkness?"*

Common Concerns Regarding Union with Christ

Couples tend to need improvement in the following areas:

- Disagreement on core spiritual issues or beliefs.

- Minimizing the importance of their spiritual differences or their partner's low level of commitment to God.

- A willingness to live separate spiritual lives without fully considering the impact this is likely to have on their relationship and children.

Navigational Aids

- Have you experienced any tension in your relationship because of differences in your spiritual beliefs?

- How do your spiritual beliefs bring you closer as a couple or push you apart?

- How do you think your spiritual beliefs will help your relationship grow stronger as you face the trials of life together?

- Are your spiritual beliefs playing a major role in your commitment to each other?

"...those who marry will face many troubles in this life..."

(1 Corinthians 7:28)

Chapter 1

In-Flight Checklist

- Discuss the specific steps you are taking and will take to build spiritual intimacy in your marriage.

- After taking some time to adjust to married life, what are some ways you could cultivate spiritual intimacy through serving others together?

- Have you given thought to how being dependent on God will affect you during difficult times?

Chapter 2
The Biblical Roles of Husbands and Wives
Learning Objectives

After this session you will be able to:

- More confidently discuss biblical roles in marriage.
- Identify and discuss non-biblical views that can lead to isolation in marriage.
- Specific steps you can take to learn and grow more in this area.

Introduction

- What are some ways that marriage roles have been confused and misused historically? Why is this so?
- What did you see in your family of origin?
- Think about the early years of your marriage. How did you work out roles in your own marriage?
- What were they based on?
- Was it easy or challenging to do?
- If it was challenging for you, what factors made it so?
- What have you learned about the wisdom of God's Word through the process?
- Why is understanding our roles and responsibilities important?

We each come into marriage with certain expectations, often based on our family-of-origin and our culture. When these expectations don't align, conflict ensues.

In many marriages, including Christian marriages, selfishness, passivity, abuse and failure to follow the example of Jesus Christ have distorted the way men and women have related to each other.

Why is this topic important?

1. **Egalitarian (Feministic):** There is no innate distinction between the roles of men and women in the home or the church.
2. **Complementarian (Moderate):** Men and women are partners in every area of life and ministry. While equal in worth, men and women have distinct and complementary gender roles in both the home and church.
3. **Hierarchical (Chauvinistic):** Women are not only commanded to follow male leadership, but are not given a voice with male leaders. Here, women are often chauvinistically kept under thumb in this polar opposite of egalitarian feminism.

Our view on marriage is Complementarian; that God designed and defined the roles in marriage for the purpose of representing a "bigger story" and to complement each other. This is the "mystery" that Ephesians 5:32 and 3:9 refers to. That the love and order in our marriages and in the Church is intended to reflect the wisdom of God to every being that God has created.

This view also recognizes the distinctiveness of male and female designed and implied purpose (role) as stated in Genesis 1:27.

The Foundations for Roles

The primary biblical roles and responsibilities in marriage aren't cultural, but are rooted in the:
- Order of creation of man and woman (Genesis 2)
- Primary responsibility and accountability for the decisions made by the marriage unit (Genesis 3:9, 17, Romans 5:12-21)
- Marital consequences mentioned in Genesis 3:16
- Relationship between Christ and the Church (Ephesians 5:32)

To understand our biblical roles in marriage, we must first understand what marriage is intended to represent.

By anchoring the roles of husbands and wives in creation and in Christ relationship to the Church, God's Word shows that these primary roles are not based on culture.

Adam sinned in two ways in the garden:
1. He defied God's command when he "ate from the tree about which I commanded you" (Genesis 3:17)

2. Passively failed to exercise his leadership, "because you listened to your wife (in conflict with God's command) and ate..." (Genesis 3:17).

God calls out Adam's disobedience as THE pivotal factor in the fall of the human race—NOT Eve's and NOT theirs jointly. There are consequences that both had to face, but even those are spoken of differently in Genesis 3:16-19

What Does the Bible Say?

- **Song of Songs 2:15** "Catch for us the foxes, the little foxes that ruin the vineyards, our vineyards that are in bloom."

- **Job 1:8-9** "Then the LORD said to Satan, "Have you considered my servant Job? There is no one on earth like him; he is blameless and upright, a man who fears God and shuns evil. Does Job fear God for nothing?" Satan replied. "Have you not put a hedge around him and his household and everything he has?"

- **Matthew 20:26-27,** "…whoever wants to become great among you must be your servant, and whoever wants to be first must be your slave."

- **Proverbs 12:15,** "The way of a fool seems right to him, but the wise man listens to advice."

- Proverbs 19:20, "Listen to advice and accept instruction, and in the end you will be wise."

Types of Roles

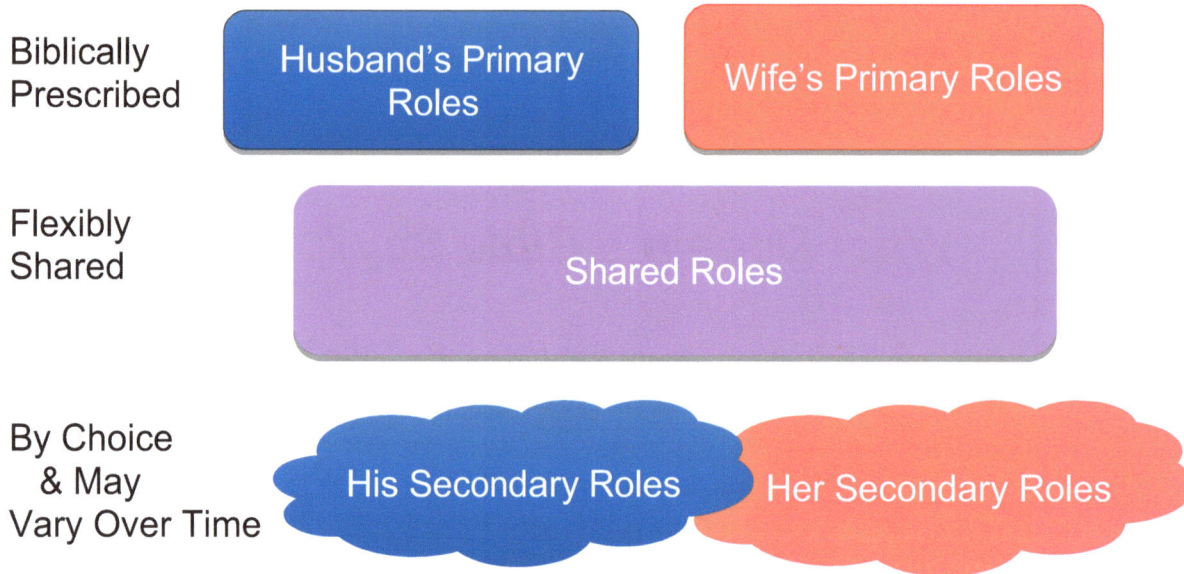

Christians are called to "not conform to this age, but to be transformed by the renewing of their mind" (Romans 12:1-2)

Role Priorities
1. Primary roles are biblically prescribed roles are intended to be consistent, unless there is a major factor involved (e.g. absence of a partner, illness, etc.)
2. Shared roles vary by a couple's abilities, interests, skills, availability, etc.
3. Secondary roles vary couple-to-couple and also over the course of a person's life as their family's needs change.

The key here is to lovingly fulfill our roles to honor God, be an example for the world as we model the relationship between Christ and His Church, and to keep the proper priorities in our lives when facing tradeoffs between the demands of different roles.

Chapter 2

Primary Roles

- The judgment and consequences of the fall extends to the primary roles for both husband and wife (Genesis 3:17-19).
    - For him, frustration would accompany his primary role as provider for his family.
    - For her, pain in childbirth and a desire to resist her husband's leadership would mark her primary roles as a wife and a mother.

God has made men and women remarkably different, yet each is also an immeasurable representation of the image of God. We are both the amazing handiwork of our loving God! His intent is that a husband and wife would complement and complete each other with the weaknesses of each bringing out the strength of the other.

If we were to add up the strengths and weaknesses of the husband, and do the same for the wife, they would both have equal value. If we were to add the two lists together, they would be a synergistic compliment to each other.

For example, the brain and the heart perform different roles, but if one fails to function properly, neither can the other. They are not the same in function or duty, but both are equally necessary for survival.

The Meaning of Marriage

- God intended that marriage would faithfully portray his love relationship with his church.
    - "This (marriage) is a profound mystery--but I am talking about Christ and the church." (Ephesians 5:32)
- To understand God's design for marriage, we must first understand how Jesus and his Church relate to each other.
    - The husband models the servant leadership of Christ (Matthew 20:25-26)
    - The wife modeling the trusting, faithful submission offered by the Church (2 Corinthians 10:5b) in joyful appreciation.

The use of the word "mystery" in the Bible means "something that has not previously been fully revealed" to us.

While some have tried to find obscure meanings for the Greek word "hupotasso," it is used in each of these verses and widely used throughout Scripture to mean "be subject to," "submit to," or to "place oneself under."

Wives are able to submit to their husbands more easily when husbands love their wives with the self-sacrificing love that Christ exemplified on earth. Likewise, husbands more naturally show love and affection toward their wives when the husbands feel respected and valued.

What are some of the consequences for a culture that doesn't know or accept God's design for marriage?
- Role confusion in marriages
- Lacking or distorted role models
- Alternative relationships replacing marriage (homosexual relationships, singles intentionally having children outside marriage)
- Confusion within the Church (e.g. female pastors and teachers of men)

Chapter 2

His Primary Roles & Responsibilities

1. Growing in his commitment to Jesus Christ as Lord of his life and as the One to whom he is accountable.
2. Practicing the spiritual disciplines (Bible study, prayer, worship, confession, repentance, etc.) so that his walk with Christ is strong, and he is fully able to be led by the Holy Spirit.
3. Providing moral (Genesis 3:9) and spiritual leadership (Ephesians 5:26-27, 29) to his family, teaching them God's Word, helping to cultivate their maturity in Christ, and setting the example for his family through his devotion to Christ.
4. Living righteously so that his family will benefit from his prayers. (1 Peter 3:12)
5. Guarding his heart from any type of inappropriate attachment with other women. (Proverbs 2:16-19, 5:1-8, 6:23-29, 7:25-27, 22:14)
6. Protecting his wife and family from Satan and spiritual attack and leading them in a God-glorifying direction to serve His purposes, not his own.
7. Developing a clear, biblical vision of mature femininity and a deep respect towards it by honoring and treating his wife as a co-heir with Christ (Romans 8:17, 1Peter 3:7) and as his partner in life. (Genesis 1:27)
8. Preparing his bride for Christ. He is called to act like Christ in her life and also for Christ in her life. (Ephesians 5:27-28)
9. Overall responsibility for the management of his family (1 Timothy 3:4-5) and supporting the instruction of his children while not provoking them to anger. (Ephesians 6:4, Colossians 3:21)
10. A willingness to lay down his life for his wife and family in any way necessary (e.g. putting their needs ahead of his own per Ephesians 5:25-27) with enduring love. (Titus 2:2)
11. Taking responsibility for establishing an environment of active listening and careful consideration of her ideas, while not lording his authority over her. (2 Corinthians 1:24)
12. Taking the initiative, having the strength, and making the sacrifice to provide for the good of his wife and children. (Luke 22:26, Ephesians 5:23, 25, 1 Timothy 5:8)
13. Interacting with his wife with a tender and sensitive heart, respectfully honoring her as the weaker (physical, emotional and/or in authority) partner (1 Peter 3:7, Colossians 3:19), and exhibiting self-control. (Titus 2:2)
14. Continually learning about and being alert to the deep needs of his wife (emotional, physical, and spiritual), and ministering to her with a

      combination of strength and tenderness. (1 Peter 3:7)
15. Conquering pride, fear, laziness, self-pity, and confusion while rejecting passivity in his responsibilities and family activities. Planning ahead in order to shepherd his family through trials that come along.
16. Accepting the burden of responsibility for making the final decision when there are disagreements.
17. Leading in the discipline of his children when both he and his wife are present. (Titus 1:6)

John Piper refers to the biblical role of men as "mature masculinity," and defines it as the "benevolent responsibility…to lead, provide for and protect…"

This includes demonstrating integrity in everything, purity in heart, mind, speech and conduct, and accepting responsibility.

This is based on the servant-leadership example of Christ.

Each has equal spiritual worth (Galatians 3:28, Luke 13:16).
Mature Femininity: is described by John Piper as "a freeing disposition to affirm, receive, and nurture strength and leadership from worthy men…"

He is to do this in a way that honors both husband and wife while leveraging their collective wisdom for married (and family) life

As the leader, he is the one who serves. A Christian husband is to follow the example of Jesus by being willing to suffer for his wife, not make her suffer for him.

This is modeled after the ministry of Christ and the work of the Holy Spirit in the Church.
This follows the model of Christ with the Church.

Outside the home, he is also responsible for utilizing his spiritual gifts to lead and serve the Body of Christ and others in his world.

Chapter 2

Her Primary Roles & Responsibilities

1. Growing in her commitment to Jesus Christ as Lord of her life and as the One to whom she is accountable and her ultimate designer and protector.
2. Practicing the spiritual disciplines (Bible study, prayer, worship, confession, repentance, etc.) so that her walk with Christ is strong, and she is fully able to be led by the Holy Spirit.
3. A clear, biblical vision of mature masculinity in her husband and a deep respect for him (Ephesians 5:33).
4. Affirming the complementary role of submission in the husband-wife relationship (1 Peter 3:1, Ephesians 5:24, Colossians 3:18, Titus 2:5) that God designed from the beginning (Genesis 3:16).
5. Embracing (a matter of action and attitude) her role as a "suitable helper" for her husband, using her gifts to support his leadership within the bounds of obedience to Christ, helping him fulfill his divine calling, and bringing glory to God (Genesis 2:18, Proverbs 12:4, Ephesians 5:25-29).
6. A non-directive approach to influencing her husband. (1 Samuel 25:23-35)
7. A winsome and affirming spirit towards her husband and recognizing that through her own weakness, her husband's strength is highlighted. This should be characterized by a "gentle and quiet spirit which is of great worth in God's sight." (1 Peter 3:4)
8. *A disposition to yield to her husband's guidance and a desire to follow his leadership out of reverence to Christ (Ephesians 5:21, Titus 2:5), "as fitting in the Lord" (Colossians 3:18), "with respect" (Ephesians 5:33), and "in everything." (Ephesians 5:24)*
9. *Managing her household well. (Proverbs 31, Titus 2:5, 1 Timothy 5:14)*
10. *Faithfully loving her husband and children. (Titus 2:4-5)*
11. *Providing for the needs of her family in various ways within and outside the home. She is to be faithful to her primary calling of caring for the family (Titus 2:4-5) while also being able to utilize her gifts and talents outside the home during the different stages of her married life. (Proverbs 31)*
12. *A willingness to wait for the rewards of her labor that will become evident in the lives of her children as they grow older and from the Lord in eternity.*

NOTE: We have made a revision to this list from the original text in The Solution for Marriages.

"Submission is the attitude of your heart that says, 'I respect you as my husband and acknowledge the leadership that God has called you to in our marriage. I want to keep myself arranged behind that leadership, to follow your lead and to partner with you as we move along our marriage journey together. I submit to God first, and he has asked me to submit myself to you. I do so willingly and in much the same manner I do this unto Jesus in my spiritual journey.'" (Scott. "WoW - Love, Respect and Submission")

surrenderedmarriage.org/2011/06/wow-love-respect-and-submission.html?utm_source=feedburner)

An example of this approach to influence is found in 1 Samuel 25:23-35, where we see Abigail respectfully appealing to her husband to get him to change his mind (Also includes cultural norms).

Neglecting this approach often leads to passivity or anger on the part of the husband.

In her personal ministry, she is called to utilizing her spiritual gifts to serve the Body of Christ, teaching younger women (Titus 2:3-5), and serving others (Acts 18:26, Romans 16:1).

This is a practical reality of parenting, where a mother's reward often comes after her children are grown.

Shared Roes of Husbands & Wives

1. Serving one another in love. (Galatians 5:13)
2. Not depriving each other sexually. (1 Corinthians 7:3-5)
3. Interdependence (1 Corinthians 11:11).
4. Working towards mutually satisfactory decisions after discussion, prayer, and seeking the guidance of God's Word.
5. Teaching their children to honor and obey God. (Ephesians 6:4)
6. As members of the church, you are called to submit to one another (Ephesians 5:21), be devoted to each other, and honor one another above yourself (Romans 12:1)

Proverbs 22:6 provides a general principle that says, *"Train a child in the way he should go, and when he is old he will not turn from it."*

Secondary Roles

- Examples of secondary roles may include:
  - A second job (him) or a job in addition to the one at home (her).
  - Starting a business.
  - Helping extended family and friends.
  - A responsibility at church or with another organization.
  - Routine tasks around the home or yard.

Discuss other possible roles.

There is room for freedom and grace for couples to prayerfully define where they draw their boundaries. These may also vary from couple-to-couple due to extenuating circumstances (e.g. illness, military deployment, stage of life, etc.).

Focus on the understanding of what marriage represents and the intent of the couple's hearts.

Principles Related to Roles

1. Any successful group has only one person ultimately responsible. (President of a country, CEO of a corporation.) In order to succeed, the leader must also have the corresponding authority.
2. If a wife usurps her husband's responsibility without God-given authority, the husband will tend to become passive at home and everyone suffers.*
3. God has given husbands both responsibility and the corresponding authority to lead and for their marriages and homes to succeed.
4. The husband will have to give an account to God for how he fulfilled this responsibility and the wife will also give an account of how she fulfilled her responsibilities.**
5. Avoid imbalance. God designed these roles to complement one another, and one role is incomplete without the other. Problems can easily arise if the roles are not clearly defined, are too rigid, or if one or both of the spouses isn't being accountable for taking care of his or her responsibilities.

*2. The desire for a wife to rule over her husband comes from the curse in Genesis 3:16 and is something that wives need to guard against.

**4. If he operates without a deep sense of responsibility before God, he will become an intolerable "monster" in the home. If a husband neglects his relationship with God, everyone suffers.

Issues Regarding Roles in Marriage

Most couples have been negatively influenced in one or more of the following areas:
- A dysfunctional family of origin.
- Poor role models who didn't follow biblical teaching.
- Television personalities and "experts."
- Social media, friends and co-worker

What other sources of influence have impacted you or others you know?

Navigation Aids

1. When there are conflicts between your roles and family responsibilities, how do you plan to manage making the final decision?
2. How will you handle headship and submission in your marriage?
3. How do you plan on handling the work responsibilities inside and outside the home? Before having children? After children arrive?
4. What type of decisions will you each make independently or only after consulting each other?
5. How do you feel about the biblical roles presented in the chapter on Roles in Marriage? Are there areas that you struggle or disagree with?

In-Flight Checklist

1. What does it mean to be a Proverbs 31 wife?
    a. What roles did she play over the course of her life as a wife and mother?
    b. Do you think she did them all at the same time?
2. What does it mean to be a Proverbs 31 husband?
3. What type of marriage do you think these two had? Why?

Note: Point to Proverbs 31:11, 12, 23 and 28.
How do you think each person played a key role in the success of the other? Who ultimately benefitted from this support and cooperation?

Note that Proverbs 31 is primarily an overview of the full life of a wise wife and mother. It's NOT the job description of Superwoman (trying to do it all at once).

1. Some questions for him to consider:
   - Examine how you have been seeking to lead.
   - Have you been a servant leader?
   - Are you leading with love?
   - Is your motivation to control or dominate your wife or to protect and care for her?
   - Consider what might be causing her reluctance to follow you.
   - Are there any unresolved issues of trust?
   - Is there abuse in her past that makes it difficult for her to yield to you?
   - Has she had teaching that promotes androgyny (no difference between men and women)?

2. Some questions for her to consider:
   - Are you demonstrating a respectful attitude towards your husband? Does he think you are?
   - Are you showing him your quiet spirit and allowing your life to speak to him?
   - Are you genuinely applauding even his smallest efforts or initiative in this area?
   - Are you resisting the urge to "take over" the leadership role?

Husbands are called to love their wife as Christ loves the church. Jesus is our role model for leadership. His example of leadership includes inviting us to follow Him, laying down his life for us, and leading us to the will of his Father.

Explain to your wife that you want to have a biblical marriage and that includes a God-given authority for you. Emphasize that this is not about who is greater, smarter or more capable. It's the scriptural teaching on this matter and a matter of godly responsibility before God. Ask her to work with you as you take these steps together.

Chapter 3
Communicating
The Control Tower is Calling
Learning Objectives

After this session you will be able to:

- *Confidently use communication skills with your spouse.*
- *Identify common areas where couples struggle with communication.*
- *Learn specific steps you can take to improve your communication and active listening skills.*

Chapter 3

Introduction

"Spend less time earning a living and more time earning a loving."

- What's the most common problem in marriages (or any relationship)?
    Poor communication
- Why is communication so difficult at times?
- Different communication styles
    Gender differences (primary need for love vs. respect)
    Defensive listening and fallout from past conflicts
    Emotions
    Selfishness and immaturity
    Fears (conscious/sub-conscious)

Why is this topic important?

- Communication is the one_____that defines every relationship. It impacts all aspects of it.

- Couples typically resist discussing _____ _____ because they do not want to create problems or start arguments.

- Ignored feelings lead to_____, _____, and a lack of_____the relationship.

- _____who wait too long to discuss what is bothering them gradually become_____toward each other.

What Does the Bible Say?

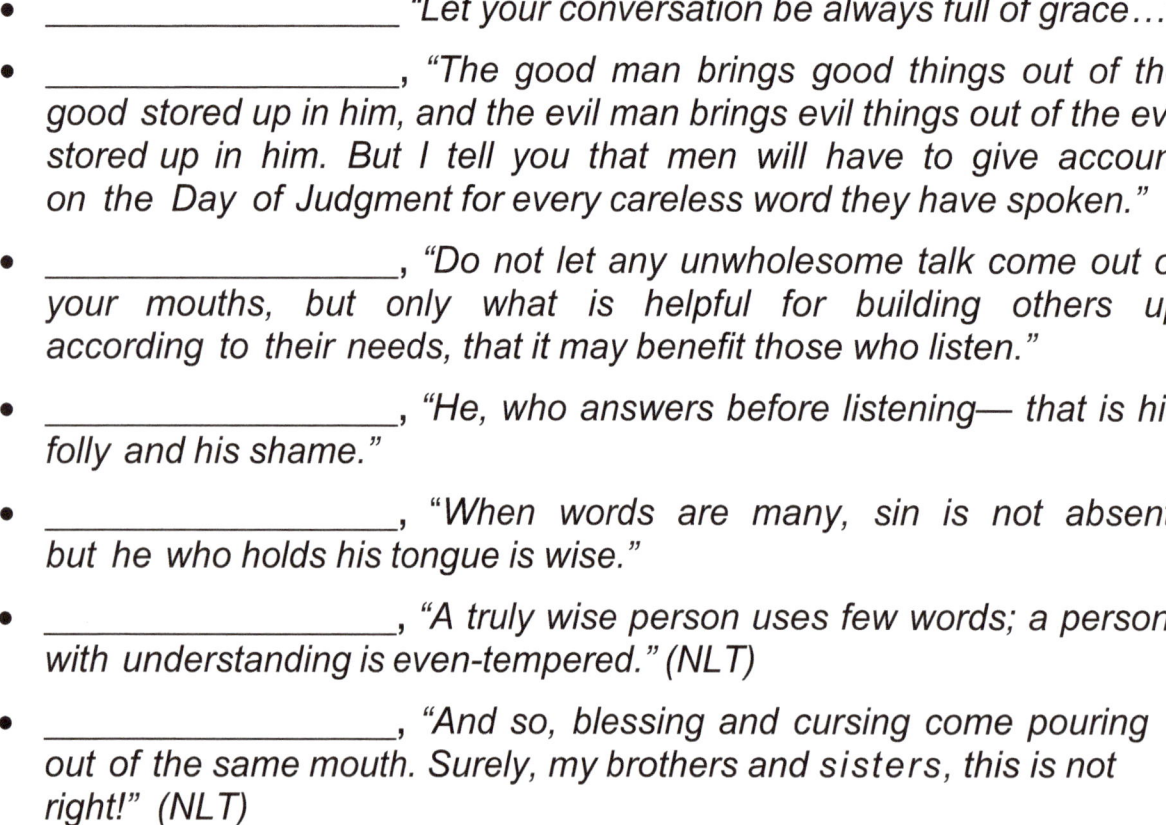

- _____ "Let your conversation be always full of grace…"
- _____, "The good man brings good things out of the good stored up in him, and the evil man brings evil things out of the evil stored up in him. But I tell you that men will have to give account on the Day of Judgment for every careless word they have spoken."
- _____, "Do not let any unwholesome talk come out of your mouths, but only what is helpful for building others up according to their needs, that it may benefit those who listen."
- _____, "He, who answers before listening— that is his folly and his shame."
- _____, "When words are many, sin is not absent, but he who holds his tongue is wise."
- _____, "A truly wise person uses few words; a person with understanding is even-tempered." (NLT)
- _____, "And so, blessing and cursing come pouring out of the same mouth. Surely, my brothers and sisters, this is not right!" (NLT)

Chapter 3

Common Concerns Regarding Communicating

Couples tend to need improvement in the following areas:

- Not believing_____their partner says.
- Making comments that_____or_____each other.
- Having difficulty_____needs and_____with each other.
- Having difficulty sharing_____ _____with each other.
- Not_____to each other_____.
- Getting_____every time someone_____with them.
- Being more interested in_____who is to blame rather than _____for_____.

Discussion Starters

1. Has your partner been a good_____and been able to _____his or her feelings about_____issues?
2. If it has been_____to share your_____with your partner, what are some things you could do to_____ communication?
3. What could your partner do (or not do) to_____you to feel heard? What_____you from finding good_____to your differences?
4. Do you typically feel_____while discussing problems with your spouse?
5. Is it usually_____for you to_____others for what _____ want?

Identifying a Couple's Primary Communication Style

- Every person should identify his or her core communication _____ by completing the Communications Style Assessment.
- A full-size download-able copy can be obtained from
  http://themarriage-journey.com/free-downloads.html

Chapter 3

Identifying & Interpreting the Results

- Check the box for each statement that most closely reflects how they respond when under a _____ amount of pressure or stress.
- What style had the _____ score?
- Was there more than one style with high scores?

Communication Style (Weights)	Always (9)	Often (6)	Sometimes (3)	Rarely (1)	Never (0)
Section 1					
Stay quiet usually and don't express what I sense.					
Seek ways to keep away from the other person					
Quickly offer an admission of guilt.					
Be hesitant to wrestle for my opinion.					
Speak softly and patiently wait for my turn to speak.					
Avoid eye contact, or twist away from the other individual.					
Believe the other person's desires or demands are much more significant than mine.					
View myself as the origin of the disagreement.					
Feel powerless, disrespected, or angry.					
Dread that I will be discarded.					
Attempt pleasing the other person despite how it might affect me individually.					
				TOTAL 1	
Section 2					
Emphasize my position, believing it is usually superior.					
Slight the other person or their contrasting viewpoint					
Fell spirited and view my opinion as triumphant when I win the dispute.					
"Stare down" or look down at the other person.					
Elevate my tone of voice in order to get my line of reasoning across.					
Regard my perception as the best solution.					
On occasion feel sorrow or responsibility over the strategy I used to succeed.					
Consider the other person's standpoint as ridiculous, stupid, or unsupported.					
Disregard the other person's wishes.					
Command the path the conversation takes.					
Guard my rights while seeking to triumph at any price.					
				TOTAL 2	

Section 3						
Fall short of my assurances due to situation beyond my control.	3					
Find it challenging to admit responsibility for disappointing others.						
Feel entitled to get my own way, even if it conflicts with "commitments" I have made to others.						
Not feel fully to blame for the measures that I undertake.						
Dread I will be disregarded if I was pushier.						
Be afraid of argument with others.						
Want my own way, without having to be accountable.						
Feel offended by what others demand from me.						
Concede to others hastily, just so I don't have to deal with the problem any longer.						
					TOTAL 3	

Adapted from The Solution for Marriages

Four Common Communication Styles

   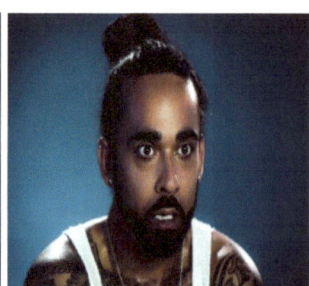

The four communication styles are:

1. _____

2. _____

3. _____

4. _____

Chapter 3

How Did Jesus Communicate?

What communication _____ did Jesus use in these situations?

- When healing others under the watchful eye of the priests and Pharisees. (Luke 17: 12-14, Matt. 12:22-23, John 9:1-7, 11:1-44)
- With his disciples in Gethsemane. (Luke 22:46, Mark 3:1-5)
- Jesus' response when he is illegally slapped at his trial (John 18:19-23)
- With the priests when discussing the woman caught in adultery (John 8:4- 5)
- When Jesus said, "I didn't come to bring peace but a sword." (Matthew 10:34)
- Clearing the money changers from the temple (John 2:13-16)
- Calling the religious leaders "a brood of vipers" (Matt. 12:34)
- When questioned by Pilate and when falsely accused while on trial. (Isaiah 53:7)
- Jesus telling the rich young man to sell what he has given to the poor and follow me. (Mark 10:21)

What about Passive-Aggressive?

Photo by Kate Remmer on Unsplash

- Did Jesus ever use the _____ communication style?
- Is it ever _____ to use a Passive-Aggressive style of communication? Why or why not?

37

The Impact on Intimacy

Communication patterns & Level of Intimacy				
Communication Pattern		**Results**		
Person A	Person B	Relationship	Who wins?	Level of Intimacy
Passive	Passive	Devitalized	Both Lose	Low
Passive	Aggressive	Dominating	I win, you lose	Low
Aggressive	Aggressive	Conflicted	Both Lose	Low
Assertive	Passive	Frustrated	Both Lose	Low
Assertive	Aggressive	Confrontational	Both Lose	Low
Assertive	**Assertive**	**Vitalized/ Growing**	**Both WIN**	**HIGH**

Source: Adapted from The Solution for Marriages

How Threats & Anxiety Drive Our Response

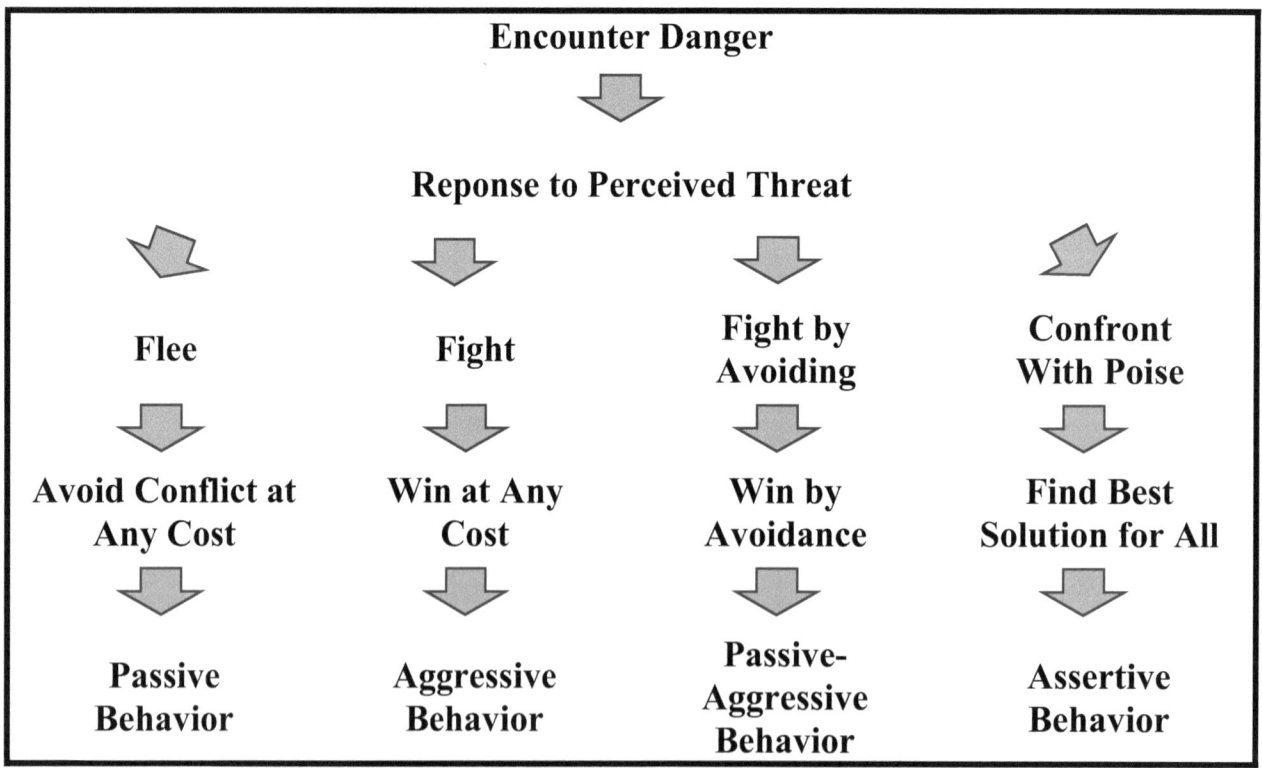

Source: Adapted from The Solution for Marriages

Chapter 3

How to be More Assertive

If you tend towards passivity:

- _____ your value before God and in your marriage!
- Don't deny or ignore _____ issues. Your _____ can be an unloving act.
- Your _____ don't have to be perfect. Move ahead, speak out and assert yourself.
- Don't _____ for speaking _____. Be as persistent as is necessary.
- Make sure your _____ matches your _____ words.

If you tend towards aggressiveness:

- Don't _____ your partner's motives. Actively _____ and show more respect.
- Attack _____ without attacking the other _____.
- Use "____" statements vs. "____" statements.
- Avoid using _____ ("You always…" or "You never…")
- Realize that every _____ does not have to be solved nor addressed.
- Recognize that _____ is the Lord's and he will make things right.

Don't be Overly Assertive

If you over use assertiveness:

- Realize that every _____ doesn't have to be approached _____.

When to get assertively involved and when not to:

- Is this a real _____ or a matter of _____?
- Is this the right _____ and _____ to address this issue?
- Is some _____ or _____ likely if I address this?
- Am I willing to take the ____ and the ____ in order to help _____ change?
- Are you _____ with the right motives?

Active Listening

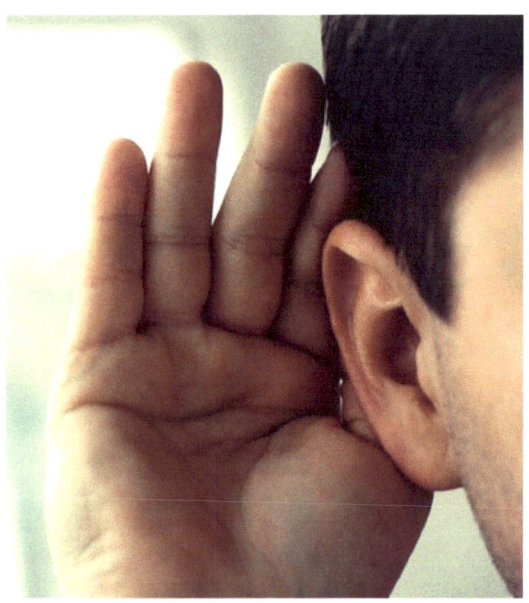

- _____ communication in marriage also requires good listening.
- Communication is about the _____ taken and being _____.

"Being heard is so close to being loved that for the average person they are almost indistinguishable."

~David Augsburger

Practice the Three Steps to Better Communication

Mirroring
- Using "I" language, one person (the Sender) makes a statement that conveys his or her thoughts, feelings, or experiences to the other person (the Receiver) such as: "I feel," "I love," or "I need."

Validation
- Validation can be challenging, especially if one's partner has a very different perspective on things.

Empathy
- In the empathy step, you want your spouse to imagine what you may be feeling, such as anger, sadness, loneliness, fear, joy, and so on.

Chapter 4
Conflict Resolution – Navigating Turbulence
Learning Objectives

After this session you will be able to:

- Understand the process of Conflict Resolution.
- Identify common conflict resolution pitfalls where you are vulnerable.
- Learn specific steps you can take to resolve conflict well.

Introduction

- What factors determine if a conflict will help or hurt a relationship?
- How does conflict help a relationship?
- How would you use the following verse to handle conflict?

"Don't let the sun go down on your anger."
Ephesians 4:26

Why is this topic important?

- Every human_____involves times of conflict – including marriage.
- Occasional_____in_____is both normal and inevitable. We all have a sin nature.
- Most couples don't deal with conflict _____.
  Because they haven't been taught_____to.

What Does the Bible Say?

- _____, "…those who marry will face many troubles in this life…"
- _____, "In your anger do not sin": Do not let the sun go down while you are still angry…" NOTE: The timing for resolving conflict is given as guidance; this is *not* a legalistic requirement!
- _____, "Do not let any unwholesome talk come out of your mouths, but only what is helpful for building others up according to their needs, that it may benefit those who listen.."
- _____, "Reckless words pierce like a sword, but the tongue of the wise brings healing."
- _____, "A gentle answer turns away wrath, but a harsh word stirs up anger..."
- Which ones would you most likely use in your conflict resolution? How?
- What other verses might you use?

Chapter 4

Discussion Starters

1. When you were growing up, how was conflict handled by your _____? Do you agree with the approach they took? Why or why not?
2. What approach do you typically use for_____ _____with your partner?
3. When you are_____, are you more likely to want to solve the problem _____away, or do you need_____to think about it?
4. Do you prefer to_____ _____in order to avoid hurting each other?
5. How does it make you feel to leave your_____?
6. As the spiritual leader of the home, what responsibility do _____ have in making sure that marital _____and problems are properly addressed? What is the_____responsibility in this?

Common Issues Regarding Conflict Resolution

Couples tend to need improvement in the following areas:

- One partner not taking _____seriously.
- Having major disputes over_____issues.
- Some differences never getting_____.
- One person tending to give in too quickly just to_____.
- Partners disagreeing on the best way to_____.

43

"The Problem" Isn't the Real Problem

Common misunderstandings include:

- Happiness is not the _____ of _____, but the ability to cope with it.
- Conflict is a _____ and _____ part of human relationships. (1 Cor. 7:28)
- As you become closer, your _____ inevitably will cause some _____. Closer relationships offer more opportunities for anger to arise than _____ relationships do.
- Conflict can be _____ to a relationship if it is handled and resolved in a _____ way.
- Conflict _____ has a strong connection with marital unhappiness.
- Anger (a "secondary emotion") is usually a _____ of another issue in the relationship that needs to be addressed.

Resolving Conflict has Two Components

- _____ Component
  - Defeating our own selfishness
- _____ Component
  - Knowing, accepting and adjusting to our differences

Chapter 4

Resolving Conflict Well

1. _____ yourself from the situation and take time to think through your anger. Clarify your own thoughts, feelings and, preferences. Ask, "What's the real issue here?" and, "What do I want to see changed?"

2. _____ on what you desire from the relationship and how that can be achieved. In the _____ situation, needs are met on both sides. It doesn't necessarily mean compromising.

3. Don't _____ in moments of anger, fatigue, hunger, low blood sugar, etc.

4. Focus solely on the _____ and _____ issue.

5. Deal with the _____ issues, rather than just the _____ that took place. To get to the root issue, ask a few times, "Why do you feel that way?"

6. Be _____ about identifying the _____ of your feelings and then discuss it calmly and confidently with your spouse.

7. Just as with a physical illness or mechanical problem, the sooner you _____ the _____, the easier it will be to fix it.

8. _____ and acknowledge that problems are rarely the fault of only one person.

9. Share both _____ and _____ feelings.

10. Be _____. Help the other person feel understood when they raise an issue. Behave in a way that _____ sharing of feelings and opinions during disagreements.

11. Work towards finding _____ while also accepting that you will not agree on everything. _____ (restraint with patience) is an act of love.

45

12. Take_____ seriously and give them the attention they deserve.

13. Speak the truth in a loving manner. Remember to examine you_____ _____. Would *you* be able to receive it if someone came to you in this manner?

14. Deal with anger and hurt_____. Don't deny it, suppress it, or let it turn to bitterness.

15. End each fight with asking for and granting_____ and doing some act of love together.

10-Steps to Resolving Conflict

1. Pick a good_____ and_____ have the discussion.

2. _____ about the situation.

3. Define the_____ or issue of _____

4. Discuss how_____ of you_____ to the problem.

5. _____ several possible ways to resolve the conflict.

6. _____and_____the pros and cons for each of these possible solutions.

7. _____, compromise,_____, and then agree upon a plan of action to try.

8. Discuss and agree on how you_____will _____ towards making this solution work.

9. Set a date and time to_____how well the selected_____ has worked. Revise your approach if necessary.

10. _____each other as you each contribute to resolving the problem.

Conflict Resolution Style

_____– Seeks to create connections so you can become more intimate and close; tends to feel rejected if partner wants more space, leading you to pursue more intensely.

_____– Tends to be emotionally distant; has difficulty showing vulnerability and dependency; manages stress by retreating into your own world and may terminate a relationship when things become too intense. Less likely to open up emotionally when you feel you are being pursued.

Emotional Intensity & Disagreement Style

	Emotional Intensity	Range of Disagreement
10	Excessive Conflict Zone	That would destroy our relationship
9		
8		I would be very upset and can't go along with that.
7	Acquiescent Zone	
6		That would be upsetting
5		
4		I don't agree and I need to explain why
3	Peaceful/Passive Zone	While I don't agree, I could live with that.
2		
1		I don't care either way.
0		I agree

Source: Adapted from The Solution for Marriages

Chapter 4

Constructive & Destructive Approaches to Conflict Resolution

Concern	Constructive Approach	Destructive Approach
Issues	Raises issues and seeks clarification	Brings up old issues (Again)
Feelings	Assertively expresses both positive and negative feelings	Expresses only negative feelings and/or uses non-assertive approach
Information	Gives complete and honest information	Only gives information that supports his/her own objectives
Approach	Attacks the issue, focusing on "common ground." Accepts shared responsibility for the outcome. Seeks "Win-Win" solution	Attacks the person, focusing on their differences and trying to change him/her. Blames the other for the problem and seeks to defeat the other person;
Change	Accepts change as a natural part of a healthy, living relationship	Stubbornly resists change by stonewalling withdrawal or avoidance.
Oneness	Finds solutions that build intimacy and trust	Loss of intimacy by escalation avoidance of difficult conversations.

Source: Adapted from The Solution for Marriages

When Couples Need Outside Help

Couples need outside help when either or both of them are:

- Feeling physically_____.
- Feeling verbally_____ or emotionally_____.
- Fighting_____ about the same issue.
- Taking your_____ out on the children.
- Using your_____ for emotional support.
- Frequent threatening_____ or_____.
- Feeling you want out of the marriage or are considering _____ on your spouse.
- Sexually_____ for a prolonged period due to relationship issues.

49

Chapter 5
Granting Forgiveness - Let God Navigate Your Heart
Learning Objectives

After this session, you will be able to:

- Confidently discuss the topic of forgiveness skills to your spouse.
- Identify common forgiveness opportunities.

Introduction

- Forgiveness is an act of_____,_____, and_____.
- Forgiveness is a_____ to not hold something against another person, despite what they have done to you.
- Forgiveness cannot be_____ _____.
- Forgiveness is neither a_____, nor_____, nor _____.

Why is this topic important?

- God_____ us to forgive. Eph 4:31-32)
- Forgiveness is a_____ promise....
- Forgiveness is a_____ to do with others what_____ did with us. (2 Cor 5:21)
- We must_____ common_____ for not forgiving.
- We don't need to feel like_____ forgiveness to do so. It's our _____. The issue is_____.

What Does the Bible Say?

- _____, "Be kind and compassionate to one another, forgiving each other, just as in Christ God forgave you."

- _____, "For if you forgive other people when they sin against you, your heavenly Father will also forgive you. But if you do not forgive others their sins, your Father will not forgive your sins."

Chapter 5

Forgiveness Myths

Some people believe that forgiveness:

- Requires an_____.
- Is an_____, one-time event.
- Means you_____have to_____the person.
- Means_____a relationship with the offender.
- Means you_____seek justice through legitimate channels.
- Requires_____the person.

Why is each of these statements untrue?

True Forgiveness

- Release him or her from_____to suffer _____or _____.
- _____, a Greek word that is often translated as "forgive."
- _____, another word for "forgive," means to give graciously, give freely, bestow.
- Releases the debt of the_____as an act of _____ to God.
- Be willing not to_____ a response when you grant forgiveness.

52

Forgiveness Is Not

- Forgiveness is not a_____. It is an_____of the_____.
- Forgiveness is not_____.
- Forgiveness is not_____.
- Forgiveness is not a form of_____.
- Forgiveness is not a sign of_____.

Forgiveness Is

- Not letting the_____off the hook.
- Returning to_____the right to take care of_____.
- Not letting the offense_____again and again.
- Not a_____; not an_____.
- Not based on_____' actions but on our_____.

Chapter 5

Four Promises of Forgiveness

- I will not_____on this incident.
- I will not bring up this_____again and use it_____you.
- I will not_____to_____about this incident.
- I will not let this incident_____ _____us or hinder our _____.

Steps to Forgiveness

- _____the pain.
- Work through_____feelings.
- Seek_____.
- Allow information to become an_____.
- Choose to_____the whole event.
- Pray_____as the Holy Spirit guides you.

Granting Forgiveness - Let God Navigate Your Heart

Learn To Forgive Yourself

- Take_____.
- Write a_____about what happened.
- Would you forgive_____ _____ for the same actions?
- Why would you_____ _____differently?
- How does it_____you to continue to_____yourself?

In-Flight Checklist

- Identify the_____and_____that directed you during the event?
- Analyze what were your_____at that time, and were they being met.
- Who are you_____to forgive?

Referrals

Today's Promise — This ministry offers mentoring and coaching designed to help those already married to enrich their relationship and for those considering marriage to prepare for the journey together.

http://www.todayspromise.org

Love and Respect — This ministry offers materials, articles, and conferences designed to help those already married to enrich their relationship and for those considering marriage to prepare for the journey together.

http://loveandrespect.com

Couple Checkup — An online marriage assessment to assist couples in discerning their strengths and growth areas.

https://www.couplecheckup.com

Marriage Alive — The Web site of Dave and Claudia Arp, a husband and wife team who strive to help couples build better marriages and families.

http://www.marriagealive.com

Chapter 6
Trust
The Flight Succeeds with Trust!
Learning Objectives

After this session you will be able to:

- Be aware that trust can always be a _____ in your marriage.
- Understand trust is the _____ that glues marriages.
- Realize trust is the _____ of what makes relationships work.

Introduction

- Trust is the _____ of what makes relationships work. It is the fundamental process of love and intimacy.
- Trust can be _____ through lies, rage, violence, drug and alcohol abuse, and, most prominently, _____ _____.
- Once trust has been lost, what can we do to _____ _____ — if anything?

Why is this topic important?

- Be on the _____
- Be _____ about your _____ and _____ feelings.
- Be _____ and _____.
- Be a spouse that keeps his/her _____.
- Be _____.
- Be aware of your partner's _____ and their best interest.

Chapter 6

What Does the Bible Say?

- _____ "But I trust in your unfailing love; my heart rejoices in your salvation."
- _____ "There is no fear in love, but perfect love casts out fear. For fear has to do with punishment, and whoever fears has not been perfected in love."
- _____ "If then you have not been faithful in the unrighteous wealth, who will entrust to you the true riches?"

5 Ways to Rebuild Trust

Couples tend to need improvement in the following areas:

- _____ _____ does work—but not completely clean.
- Being_____, righteous or casual about the problem_____ works.
- Talk about_____ made you do it.
- Be an_____.
- Renew your_____.

Trust The Flight Succeeds with Trust!

Navigational Aids

1. Communicate in real time "_____"
2. Tap into your _____ trust.
3. Don't make relationship_____ when you're _____
4. Find the_____ between gains and losses in your _____ of trust.

In-Flight Checklist

- The most important thing you can do when _____ trust in a relationship is to be_____.
- Seek to learn_____ about your partner.
- Understand the_____.
- Sincerely_____.

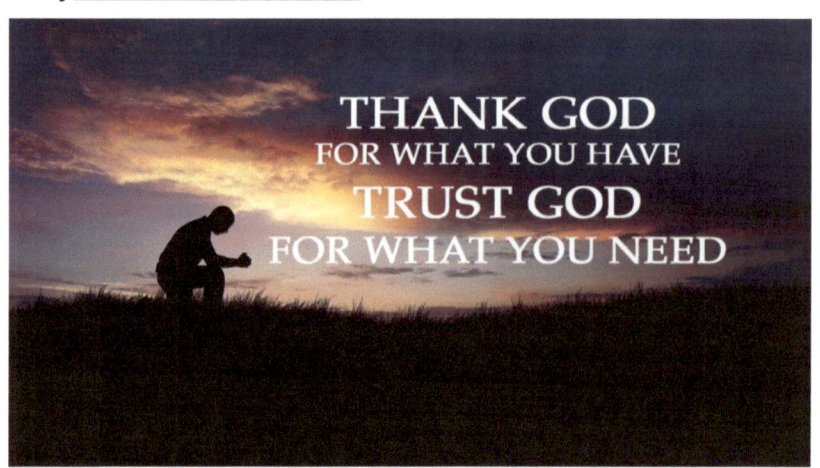

Chapter 6

Write Your Story Here

Chapter 7
The Internet, Social Media and Friends - Protecting Your Flight Path.
Learning Objectives

After this session, you will be able to:

- Confidently discuss social media issues with your spouse.
- Recognize possible danger areas where you may be susceptible.
- Assess your ability as a couple to institute the safeguards for using social media safely.

Chapter 7

Introduction

How Do You Socialize Online?

- **What** social media sites do you use?
- **Why** do you use social media?
- **Who** do you engage with? **What** boundaries have you established?
- **How** much do you use it?
- **When** do you use it?
- **Where** do you use it?
- **What** in depth steps do you presently use to safeguard your marriage when using social media?
- Are you both in harmony on what is "answerable and suitable use" of social media?

Why is this topic important?

- The Internet provides a sense of_____.
- The lack of_____ _____provides a false sense of security.
- People tailor the_____for their friends to read, forgetting

 that others may see it.
- They want to offer_____to impress_____friends or associates.

SOURCE: Protect Your Privacy: Take Control of Social Networking

"Maintaining privacy on social networks is much like hanging all your dirty laundry on a highway billboard—and then asking only your friends to look."

~ Rich Mogal ~

The Internet, Social Media and Friends - Protecting Your Flight Path.

What Does the Bible Say?

_____, "Do not be misled: "Bad company corrupts good character."

_____, "Catch for us the foxes, the little foxes that ruin the vineyards, our vineyards that are in bloom."

_____, "Then the LORD said to Satan, "Have you considered my servant Job? There is no one on earth like him; he is blameless and upright, a man who fears God and shuns evil. Does Job fear God for nothing?" Satan replied. "Have you not put a hedge around him and his household and everything he has?"

Common Concerns Regarding Social Media

Attacks and Unintended Information Disclosure
- _____
- _____
- _____
- _____
- _____

Professional and Personal Implications
- _____
- _____
- _____

Tips To Protect Your Marriage Against Social Media Pitfalls

- Be_____about your_____in contacting the other person.
- Limit the_____of your contacts.
- Don't talk_____.
- Let your_____know with whom you are connecting.
- Share your_____and_____ e-mails/texts with your spouse.
- Do not_____in person unless your_____is with you.

The Internet, Social Media and Friends - Protecting Your Flight Path.

Social Media Items to Consider

- Married couples ought to carefully consider the amount of _____ _____ they include and the details they want to provide.
- What are each partner's_____ and feelings about_____ online _____ with persons outside the circle of their marriage and immediate family?
- What are the_____ for accepting friend requests?
- Couples should share passwords and maintain an " _____ _____ to ALL of your accounts. (Phone, tablet, computer, social media)

Social Media Items to Consider

- How much_____ should you be spending on social media?
- What_____ are you still in contact with from past relationships?
- What does your social media_____ look like? Have you _____ _____ since you got married or engaged?
- Give careful thought to the number of_____ you use to access your account.
- _____ one another on social media much the same as you_____ one another at a party or social gathering.

Chapter 7

Possible Warning Signs

- Paying more_____ to his or her social media connections than to your spouse.
- _____ with others instead of talking to your _____ about a concern.
- _____ anything regarding your use of social media.
- Changes or decline in importance of _____ as a couple.

Additional Resources

US-CERT Resources:

- Staying Safe on Social Network Sites (https://www.us-cert.gov/cas/tips/ST06-003.html)

- Guidelines for Publishing Information Online (https://www.us-cert.gov/cas/tips/ST05013.html)

Other Resources

- The Dangers of Social Media
  https://turbofuture.com/internet/The-Dangers-of-Social-Networking-Why-you-need-to-be-careful

- Social Networking and Security Risks (Social Network at Work)
  https://www.gfi.com/whitepapers/Social_Networking_and_Security_Risks.pdf

- Internet Safety 101
  http://internetsafety101.org/snsdangers

Chapter 8
Intimacy In Marriage - Enjoy the Flight God's Way

Learning Objectives

After this session, you will be able to:

- Confidently discuss the topics of Intimacy
- Identify common misunderstandings that you may have about intimacy.
- Learn steps you can take to prepare for or improve intimacy in your marriage.

Introduction

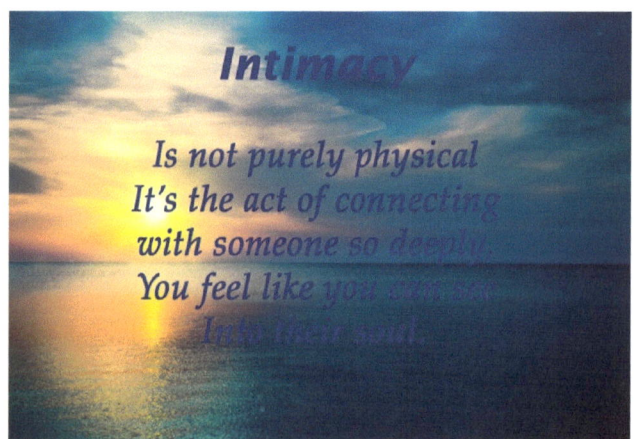

Couples are getting most of their _____ from secular sources and are forming _____ that are increasingly in conflict with God's Word.

- Historically, the Church has also _____ to the distortions (e.g. sex is distasteful, evil, or only for purposes of procreation) and even

Chapter 8

today, continues to remain generally _____ on this topic.

- As a result, couples are suffering the consequences of _____ in their lives and _____.

Why is this topic important?

It comes down to couples needing to understand God's purposes for intimacy.

- Couples often_____why God created intimacy.

- People tend to look at _____ from the perspective of _____ _____.

- Healthy_____that involves our whole being: Spiritual, Emotional, Intellectual and Sexual intimacy.

- Unfortunately, many couples bring a lot of "_____ _____" into their relationship.

What Does the Bible Say?

_____ – "Marriage should be honored by all, and the marriage bed kept pure, for God will judge the adulterer and all the sexually immoral."

_____ - "Flee from sexual immorality. All other sins a person commits are outside the body, but whoever sins sexually, sins against their own body. Do you not know that your bodies are temples of the Holy Spirit, who is in you, whom you have received from God? You are not your own; you were bought at a price. Therefore, honor God with your bodies."

Common Concerns Regarding Intimacy

Couples tend to need improvement in the following areas:

- Concerns about_____experiences that either or both parties have had.

- Dealing with different_____of intimacy or understanding the four types of intimacy.

- Discomfort talking about intimacy due to_____or lack of a mature_____knowledge.

Chapter 8

Four Types of Intimacy In Marriage

Christian marriage begins with essential truths in intimacy

1. _____ intimacy - the intensity of devotion

2. _____ intimacy - the thrill of romance

3. _____ intimacy - the honing of mind

4. _____ intimacy - the physical bliss

If you are in_____ with each of these four_____, determine if God is giving you both a sense of peace about it.

Navigational Aids

Christian marriage succeeds with essential truths

- Marriage is a covenant, not a _____, designed by God (Hosea 2:19)
- Restoration of _____ marriages is the goal (Malachi 2:13-16)
- The husband seeks to meet all the _____ of his wife and the wife seeks to meet all the _____ of the husband (Ephesians 5:25-33)
- The Bible is the decisive _____ on strong relationships—especially within the marriage (Genesis 2:24)

In-Flight Checklist

1. When you were growing up, did your parents discuss intimacy? Do you agree with the _____ they took? Why or why not?

2. What approach do you _____ use for intimacy discussion with your spouse?

3. Does intimacy mean _____ to you now than _____ this discussion? Why or why not?

Chapter 9
Marriage Expectations - The Pre-flight Experience
Learning Objectives

After this session you will be able to:

Discuss how_____your expectations are.

Understand where your_____came from by _____where the major_____ of input came from.

Discuss how we know what_____thinks about marriage.

Introduction

"When a couple is still infatuated with each other, you don't need much because you're still enjoying that chemical high. You expect very little, you feel great, and you're spending a lot of time trying to please each other. But as the relationship deepens, expectations change. And when you're not getting those needs met, suddenly your partner can do little that pleases you - everything seems annoying....You may start arguing, but not about the real issues that are bothering you."[1]

Love, Patricia, and Jo Robinson. *Hot Monogamy: Essential Steps to More Passionate, Intimate Lovemaking.* New York: Plume, 1995.

Marriage Expectations - The Pre-flight Experience

Why is this topic important?

- We all enter marriage with_____expectations that are formed through a wide variety of previous experiences and inputs from our families, culture, and the media.
- _____about love and marriage have a powerful impact on_____.
- Couples will be happy or _____in life based on how well what is happening_____up with what they think should be_____.

What Does the Bible Say?

_____
Proverbs 20:6 *"Many a man claims to have unfailing love, but a faithful man who can find?"*
Proverbs 31:26
"She speaks with wisdom, and faithful instruction is on her tongue."

_____
Colossians 3:13 *"Bear with each other and forgive whatever grievances you may have against one another. Forgive as the Lord forgave you."*

Chapter 9

Common Concerns Regarding Marriage Expectations

- Thinking the_____of new love will never change or _____.
- Not realizing that their_____will change or be uncovered during different_____of married life.
- Fear of losing their_____ _____once married.
- Concern about divorce due to_____experience or from seeing the experiences of_____.
- _____ (and low) expectations for their marriage, based on what they have seen in others (_____).

Navigational Aids

- Where did this_____(household chores, finances, etc.) come from?
- Is the expectation_____or_____?
- Did_____and_____have an impact on your trigger point?

Chapter 9

In-Flight Checklist

- Honor_____.

- Be_____, understanding, and_____of personal boundaries.

- _____provides a relationship the _____it needs to keep from ripping apart.

- Admit you are_____. An apology should not indicate _____or threat; it is a sign of _____and self-worth.

77

Chapter 10
Boundaries
Introduction

Boundaries in a relationship are similar to boundaries on your property. Without a boundary of some kind, you are more likely to have arguments or difficulties with your neighbors.

Every relationship needs to develop healthy and balanced boundaries. Without healthy boundaries in a marriage, numerous problems, hurts, and misunderstandings occur. This chapter is intended for couples encountering issues with relational boundaries.

Tips for Discussing Boundaries

Most successful couples establish their boundaries early in their relationship. During the first year of marriage, there may be power struggles as you set boundaries, rules, and responsibilities. While it is still possible, it is more difficult and often quite traumatic to change them later. It is especially hard to make changes without having ever discussed what these specific boundaries are.

Clarifying responsibilities early on enables both partners to decide on a fair distribution of responsibilities in the home. Who will be responsible for what in the relationship? It's important to be assertive about how you feel while doing it in a way that expresses love and commitment to the relationship. Christ-like service is a great way to show love to each other, but it also helps for both of you to know what is expected and what you are doing as an act of service.

Some things are duties and some things are gifts. Problems occur when one person does something as a gift while the other sees it as a duty. For example, the husband may think that the wife should take care of her own car's maintenance. If he fills the gas tank a few times and changes the oil without having discussed expectations in advance, she may feel that he is taking responsibility for maintaining her car. This creates a problem if he feels he is only doing an occasional favor for her. Thus, when the car runs out of gas or the oil light goes on, it may lead to a big fight. She may resent his failure to keep the car in order, while he feels that she didn't appreciate his kindness.

Setting personal and relational boundaries is crucial for a healthy marriage. There is a fine balance needed here. Couples need to love and sacrifice for each other while also taking care of themselves. When both parties love and watch out for each other the way God intended, these principles work together wonderfully. When the relationship is out of balance, problems will arise.

Most people inherit their problems with setting appropriate boundaries from their family of origin.

The following Family Patterns have a distinct impact on a couple's ability to set a healthy balance between closeness and flexibility in their marriage. Examine them closely with your mentees to help them determine appropriate boundaries within their relationships.

Common Patterns Found in Very Distant Families

Characteristics of distant families include:
1) Family members appear to care little for each other, while only caring about themselves.
2) "You live your life, and I'll live mine."
3) While the individuals might feel loved, it is rarely expressed verbally or by actions.
4) Members are mostly on their own for getting their needs met.

Later on, people from these families tend to continue distant and disconnected relationships. It causes their marriage to look more like a corporate merger as each pursues their own careers, hobbies, social, and leisure activities.

A possible impact on a marriage often comes right after the honeymoon phase of marriage. Suddenly, one person realizes that the other isn't the "perfect" partner. They resort to the coping behavior that they grew up with and then withdraw emotionally. This worked well when they were growing up as it protected their heart from more pain. But in a marriage, emotional withdrawal only leads to serious consequences. It's important to recognize how and why they are responding that way and help them change.

Common Patterns Found in Very Enmeshed Family Patterns

Characteristics of enmeshed families include:
1) Family members smother each other with love and affection, leading to an unhealthy dependence.
2) Family members have a hard time doing anything on their own.
3) Decision making is difficult because everything needs to be decided together—even irrelevant details.
4) Members may be emotionally punished for doing anything that excludes the whole family.
5) Moving out on your own or going away to college was particularly traumatic.

Imagine a man being depressed due to a work situation. He comes home quiet and reclusive. Being from an enmeshed family, everyone else feels they *must* know what's going on. They can even assume that it is somehow their fault and then press him to tell them everything that is bothering him. This only pushes the man further away, making matters worse.

Some enter marriage thinking that love means enjoying and doing *everything* together. When such partners feel a need to be alone for a while, they experience a deep sense of guilt. It is a concern when one person loses himself or herself in the other person or when one feels guilty for not being totally enmeshed.

In a balanced relationship, the couple enjoys sharing many moments and activities together but will also encourage each other in independent pursuits. Healthy relationships involve interdependent *and* independent activities.

Finding a healthy balance is challenging early in a marriage, if one or both parties did not experience a healthy balance growing up. Change is best approached gradually, especially when patterns are deep rooted. Give your spouse permission to let you know whenever you are responding in unhealthy ways.

Here are some questions to discuss:
1) Did you grow up with rigid boundaries or lack of appropriate boundaries? How did it affect you growing up? How does it affect your relationship now?
2) Which way do you tend to lean now: people pleaser or being too harsh?

3) What hobbies or activities infringe on the boundaries of your dating or marriage relationship?

Setting Boundaries with the Opposite Sex after Marriage
A couple being friendly with other couples is fine. It's much more sensitive, though, when you are dealing with one-on-one, opposite sex relationships. There are many people who can be impacted by inappropriate behavior, including the other person, yourself, your spouse, your children, your peers, and so forth. In these cases, extra caution is imperative.

1) Guard your communication. Don't discuss things that are personal or that you aren't fully discussing with your spouse.

2) Set cautious boundaries on your level of intimacy: physical, emotional, spiritual, and verbal.

3) Don't run to this person when you are upset, stressed or struggling in your relationship. If your marriage is struggling in small areas, even a casual friendship with someone of the opposite sex can be fraught with danger.

4) Guard your emotions. If you find yourself thinking about them or looking forward to being together, you are flirting with danger and must back away physically and emotionally. Don't be emotionally unfaithful to your spouse.

5) Guard against your being alone with this person, especially in non-public places. Leave your office door slightly or completely open. Time together should be limited and pure in purpose.

6) Keep your spouse informed before any necessary time alone with someone of the opposite sex. Review the plans in detail, and only proceed if you have your spouse's full consent. If you are lying or misleading your spouse about this person, you have already gone too far.

Discussion Starters
1) Do you feel fully accepted and respected by your partner's family and friends?
2) Do you both feel that you spend the right amount of time with each of your families and friends?

3) Do you anticipate that your family or friends will interfere with your relationship? If so, how?
4) How would you like to see your relationship with your partner's family or friends improved?
5) How do you or could you protect each other from those who would cross your relational boundaries as a couple?

Recommended Resources

Cloud, Henry, and John Townsend. Dr. *Boundaries: When to Say Yes, When to Say No.* Grand Rapids, MI: Zondervan, 1992.

Chapter 11
Navigational Cards
The Checkpoints Along the Journey

A premium resource, our Navigational Cards, can be obtained in the Resources section of *The Marriage Journey* website.

The cards serve as navigation "checkpoints" similar to most flight requirements to report their route checkpoints with flight control centers! Each deck of cards contains 54 words relative to marriage, one on every card. A scripture for that word supports each word. That word is intended to provoke discussion, thought and strength to the couple. The Navigation Cards help couples to learn where they are aligned and reveal strength in their marriage. At other times, they'll discover a word that prompts an opportunity for growth. (We call it flight path adjustment.) Together, the couple can experience joy and a better understanding of their spouse by using a simple set of cards (flight guides).

How are the cards important in your discussion? Begin by selecting twelve (12) cards that contain significant words to you on today's discussion. Once you both have selected your cards, share the results, noting any similar words. Set the cards with similar words aside for now.

Now share why you chose the words (cards), using the Assertive Communication and Active Listening skills you learned in **Chapter 2,**

Communicating - *The Control Tower Is Calling* and **Chapter 17, Marriage Expectations** - *The Pre-flight Experience*. Be sure to read and share the corresponding Scripture on each of these cards, and then tell your partner how that Scripture relates to the discussion today.

Sort the cards again, including the cards with similar words, narrowing your selection to six cards. Compare your selection with your spouse again. Once again, set aside any cards with similar words. Explore, once again, why these cards continue to be important to you in this conversation. (Don't use the same description you used above, because the reason you chose these cards have a deeper meaning to you now than a few minutes before.) Gather your cards together one more time, including the ones you set aside. Sort them again, but this time, select the single most significant word to you. Now compare this sorting result with your spouse's choice. Did you select a card with the same word or have you each chosen a unique card? These cards, and the Scriptures, are the most meaningful in your relationship at this moment. Read the verse to each other, share the word, and then discuss why you chose this single card. Speak with sincerity and love. Be sure you are not talking with a tone of aggression, distrust, or disbelief. Be positive, choose kind phrases.

Remember, the discussion and choices will differ, because the topic of discussion is never the same. (Even if the subject is similar, the discussion will change because the elements leading to the dialogue differ.) The words and Scripture for each conversation will be unique to that exchange and have a special impact on your result.

Use the cards often, in many scenarios, to help you gain a better understanding of your spouse and yourself. Combine them with the Conflict Resolution steps, Forgiveness discussions, Stress Management techniques and more.

Additional resources, updates and downloadable material is available from themarriage-journey.com/free-downloads.html

Chapter 12
Handling Cultural Differences
Learning Objectives

After this session you will be able to:

- Appreciate the specific cultural issues a multicultural couple may potentially endure.
- Understand why couples in multicultural or multiracial relationships usually have above average curiosity and excitement to learn about the others' ancestry and traditions.
- Discover how these marriages also come with greater challenges in building a lasting and fulfilled marriage.

Chapter 12

Introduction

- Intercultural marriages increased by 28 percent in the last decade.
- "Multicultural" vs. "Interracial" meanings.
    Culture – behavior
    Race - biology
- Do you have the same values and shared vision of life?

Why is this topic important?

- Intercultural marriages are_____in America.
- Such marriages have_____and such couples see high divorce rates.
- _____can result from differing cultural attitudes toward the extended family.

What Does the Bible Say?

- _____, "From one man he made every nation of men that they should inhabit the whole earth; and he determined the times set for them and the exact places where they should live."
- _____, "Just as a body, though one has many parts, but all its many parts form one body, so it is with Christ."
- _____ "There is neither Jew nor Gentile, neither slave nor free, nor is there male and female, for you are all one in Christ Jesus."

Common Concerns Regarding Culturally Different Marriages

Couples tend to need improvement in the following areas:

- Couples have to _____ different communication patterns.

- _____ on what you want for your children.
- Learn to accept new _____.
- Partners agreeing on the best way to _____ _____.

Navigational Aids

1. _____ the opportunities.
2. Learn more about your spouse's _____.
3. Look for _____.
4. Plan for your _____.

Handling Cultural Differences

In-Flight Checklist

- Prioritize your spiritual_____ as a Christ follower.
- _____ versus _____.
- _____ and _____ dicey issues.
- _____ with your in-laws.
- Be_____.
- Pray daily for_____, _____ and _____.

Source: **Focus on the Family**

Chapter 13
Married Again - The 2nd Flight, but Not Together
Learning Objectives

After this session you will be able to:

- Understand rebuilding a future after divorce is by no means an easy path.
- Recognize blended families don't 'just get along.'
- Learn specific steps create a strong, healthy blended family.

Introduction

- Blended families are not_____.
- Most couples enter into_____ with unrealistic expectations.

- Fear of _____ is part of the remarriage _____.
- The death of a spouse, marriage separation, and divorce, the _____ processes for each are similar. *

*Einstein, Elizabeth. *The Blended family: Living, Loving, and Learning.* New York: Macmillan, 1988.

Why is this topic important?

- People don't just fall in love, get married and _____ live happily ever after.
- Nearly _____ of remarriages end in divorce.*
- _____ and _____ marriages present challenges not experienced in the first.

*Popenoe, D., & Whitehead, B. D. (2007). The state of our unions 2007: The social health of marriage in America. Piscataway, NJ: The National Marriage Project. (See pp. 18–19.)

What Does the Bible Say?

- _____,"Place me like a seal over your heart, like a seal on your arm; for love is as strong as death, its jealousy unyielding as the grave. It burns like blazing fire, like a mighty flame."

- _____, "My dear brothers and sisters, take note of this: Everyone should be quick to listen, slow to speak and slow to become angry."

- _____, "Do not let any unwholesome talk come out of your mouths, but only what is helpful for building others up according to their needs, that it may benefit those who listen.."

Chapter 13

How To Prepare for Blended Families

- Recognize and deal with the _____.
- Develop a solid _____ bond.
- Deal with the _____ from your previous relationships.
- Involve the _____.
- Accept _____ shifts in the household.
- Remember, there are no _____, only _____.

Navigational Aids

Couples tend to need improvement in the following areas:

- The biological parent/child bond existed before the marriage.

- The new spouse gets an instant family upon marriage, rather than slowly through childbirth.
- Often one of the child's biological parents lives elsewhere.
- The children may have to observe visitation rights and move between homes.
- Some or even all of the new family members have already experienced loss through divorce or death.

In-Flight Checklist

Some common storms that may arise are:

- Negative reactions from stepchildren.
- How to handle holidays.
- Which church to attend.
- Contraception.
- Finances.

Chapter 13

Resources

Chapter 14
Remarriage
Introduction

Couples getting married for the first time in the United States have approximately a 45 to 50% chance of getting divorced. Remarried couples have an even greater divorce rate at about 60% with that rate increasing even more when children are involved. Why?

Compared to first marriages, remarriages tend to:
1) Involve more people with personality characteristics that are detrimental to successful marriage (e.g. selfishness, impulsivity, neuroticism).
2) Be more accepting of divorce as an option when there are marital problems.
3) Have less social support than first time marriages have.
4) Add additional pressure and baggage from the previous marriages (e.g. emotional pain, legal issues, child support, children visitation rights, etc.).

In addition, many remarried couples haven't yet learned to successfully resolve marital disagreements, and thus they are more prone to repeating behaviors that led to problems in their first marriage. This is likely to involve a greater commitment of time for all involved in the mentoring process.

Common Issues Regarding Remarriage
1) Insufficient time to heal from the prior divorce.
2) Unresolved issues or ongoing conflict with former spouse.
3) Lack of training in key marriage skills, such as communication, conflict resolution, finances, and so on.
4) Haste to get married due to loneliness, sexual temptation, and so on.
5) If this is a first marriage for one of the partners, they may be unaware of past issues or minimize them as not being relevant to their current relationship.
6) Lack of biblical justification for remarriage and wanting to remarry anyway.

Tips on Discussing Remarriage

Successful remarriages have several common characteristics. These couples:

1) Finished grieving their prior loss and are emotionally ready for this marriage. (Ongoing hostility with a former spouse indicates a problem in this area.)
2) Got pre-marital counseling or mentoring and are engaged with other groups that will provide encouragement, support, and accountability.
3) Learned from past mistakes and have a clear picture of their couple strengths and weaknesses.
4) Realistically faced the challenges ahead with reasonable expectations (e.g. adjusting to new family members and understand how challenging marriage can be).
5) Nurture their couple bond by setting time aside for themselves as a priority.
6) Start fresh in a new house and neighborhood.
7) Don't compare the new marriage with their old one.
8) Are open to personal change and relational compromise and adjustments.
9) Get financial counsel, especially when there are issues with alimony, child-support, or finances.
10) Form new routines and family traditions while flexibly adopting the best from each partner's experiences.
11) Work towards re-developing transparency and vulnerability in their marriage while openly acknowledging their hopes and fears.
12) Leave the negativity from their prior marriage behind.

Couple Exercises

Download a copy of "Questions Before Considering Remarriage" from the Resources section of TheSolutionForMarriages.com and have the couple review and discuss it together. Debrief selected areas with them.

Discussion Starters

1) Have you both discussed the Property or Marital Settlement Agreement (or Marital Separation Agreement) from the past marriage(s)?
2) What impact do you think this agreement will have on your relationship? Your children? Your finances?
3) Do you think a Pre-Marital Agreement is necessary for your relationship/marriage? Why or Why not?

Biblical References

Is there a biblical option for this remarriage? Some verses that apply to this are:
- 1) Matthew 5:31-32
- 2) Matthew 19:1-12
- 3) Mark 10:1-12
- 4) Luke 16:18
- 5) 1 Corinthians 7:10-16

Recommended Resource

Rosberg, Gary, and Barbara Rosberg. *Divorce Proof Your Marriage*. Wheaton, IL: Tyndale House, 2004.

Chapter 15
Blended Families
Introduction

Many experts agree that unrealistic expectations for blended family life often set couples up for great disappointment. While all new marriages involve different people and different dynamics, it is not uncommon for individuals to slip into the same old patterns and routines (e.g. being avoidant during conflict), especially in the midst of the stress of blending two families.

Christian blended families are becoming more and more common in our society. This chapter looks at the unique challenges that Blended families face and helps prepare the mentee couple for that.

Common Issues Regarding Blended families
1) Managing the roles and expectations of father vs. stepfather and mother vs. stepmother.
2) Couples not recognizing the level of challenge involved with integrating two families.
3) Children coming between the parent and stepparent in matters of house rules, discipline, and so forth.

Tips on Discussing Blended families

When two families form one blended family, they often struggle with the integration because they come from two different households and different sets of rules. A crucial point to the blended family success is to set up rules for discipline and be consistent with the rules for all children involved. Rules should not be permitted to be stretched or broken nor should children be permitted to maneuver one parent against another.

A blended family often experiences times when the child or children visit the noncustodial parent. As stepparents, we should strive to be good examples of godliness and manage ourselves with integrity.

Below is a list of common unrealistic and realistic expectations for both parents and children.

Common Expectations	
Unrealistic	**Realistic**
Love will happen instantly between all family members.	Love may or may not happen between blended family members. It will take time for relationships to develop; some will bond quickly, others slowly.
We'll do marriage better this time around.	Individuals who have experienced a breakup or divorce often have learned tough lessons from the past. But a new marriage cannot be compared to a prior one. It involves different people and different marital dynamics.
'Blending' is the goal of this blended family.	When relationships "blend," they are equal and everyone feels connected. It's common for couples to want their family to "blend" quickly. But the truth is, some blended family members may never "blend," while others form close bonds.
Our children will feel as happy about this new family as we do.	The truth is children will at best feel confused about the new marriage, and at worst, they'll resent it. Remarriage is a gain for adults and another loss for children, at least initially. Usually, the reason for the remarriage was to gain the potential spouse, not the children that come with that spouse. For many, stepchildren are a necessary evil.
A child's expectation: My stepparent will not try to act like my parent.	Sometimes stepparents want so badly to be accepted that they try to manage the children as a biological parent would. Unfortunately, the children will still notice the difference.
A child's expectation: When my stepparent does discipline me, they will act just like my biological parent.	What's familiar to children is their biological parent's parenting style. A different parenting style and different rules can be difficult to adjust to. Before marriage, try to

	bring each household's rules in line with each other (e.g. same bedtime, curfew, etc.). After marriage, each parent should strive to be the authority with their own children and agree to the same rules for everyone.

Source: Adapted from The Solution for Marriages

Couple Exercises

A stepmother expressed the following expectations two years into her remarriage:

1) I thought my husband would appreciate how overwhelming and difficult it would be for me to care for his children.

2) I thought that raising his children would fulfill my need to be a mother.

3) I thought I would have more say in the children's visitation schedules (e.g. when we watch them for their mother, when they spend the night at a friend's house, etc.).

4) I expected to fit in, to be welcomed by his children, and to be treated well.

5) I expected to immediately take priority over all his other relationships, even his children.

How do you identify with her desires? How realistic do you believe them to be? Discuss as a couple.

Discussion Starters
1) What have you each done to fully understand and prepare for the realities of life in a blended family?

2) What do you see as the major challenges you are likely to face in adjusting as a blended family?

3) How aware are you of the stress your couple relationship is likely to experience?

4) How much have you talked about the new and unique parenting responsibilities you will have?

5) What discipline scenarios have you discussed? Are you in agreement on discipline for your children? Your partner's children?

Additional discussion items can be found in Chapter 31, Remarriage.

Biblical References
1 Timothy 3:4, *"He must manage his own family well and see that his children obey him with proper respect."*

Titus 2:3-5, "Likewise, teach the older women to be reverent in the way they live, not to be slanderers or addicted to much wine, but to teach what is good. Then they can urge the younger women to love their husbands and children, to be self-controlled and pure, to be busy at home, to be kind, and to be subject to their husbands, so that no one will malign the word of God."

Recommended Resources
Deal, Ron L. *The Smart Stepfamily*. Minneapolis, MN: Bethany House, 2006.

Chapter 16
Becoming Full-Time Caregivers for Your Parent(s)
Flying The Historic Airplane
Learning Objectives

After this session, you will be able to:

- Understand the challenges of caregivers.
- Identify common stressors being a full-time caregiver.
- Recognize how your marriage can be affected.
- Identify ways to stay 'healthy' as a caregiver.

Introduction

- Baby boomers are the most common elder caregivers.
- 43.5 million Americans are currently caring for someone older than 50 years of age. *
- Baby boomers are the 'sandwich generation'.
- Dementia is the most common chronic disabling condition. **

   According to recent statistics provided by the Family Caregiver Alliance (FCA), an estimated 43.5 million Americans are currently caring for someone older than 50 years of age. Additionally, baby boomers are becoming the individuals who most commonly provide caregiving as well as require elder care home services themselves, as 10,000 members of the generation reach 65 every day.

**Population Reference Bureau, Today's Research on Aging, Issue 33, February 2016, http://www.prb.org/pdf16/TodaysResearchAging33.pdf

Chapter 16

Why is this topic important?

- 1 in 10 women, age 45 to 64, provides parental and financial care in their homes for one or more years. (PSID Wiemers and Bianchi (2015)
- Divorce also has implications for whether older adults will receive care from their children. (Silverstein and Giarrusso 2010)
- Unmarried women with few economic resources are likely to be particularly disadvantaged by not having a spouse to provide care. (Ryan and colleagues 2012)

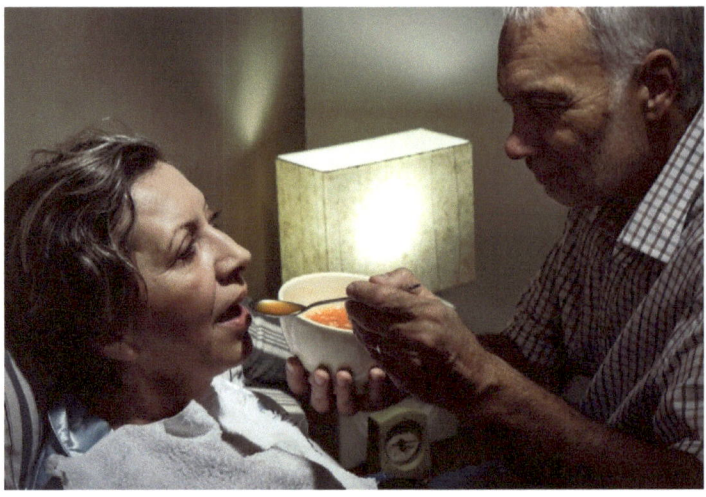

- Wives tend to be the sole care providers for their husbands. (HRS-related Asset and Health Dynamics Among the Oldest Old (AHEAD)
- Daughters are much more likely to become their mother's primary caregivers, underscoring the "primacy of the mother-daughter tie,"
  Leopold, Raab, and Engelhart (2014)
- Informal care that family and friends provide for older Americans totals an estimated $522 billion a year. Chari and colleagues (2015)

What Does the Bible Say?

_____, "Anyone who does not provide for their relatives, and especially for their own household, has denied the faith and is worse than an unbeliever."

_____, "…Then they can train the younger women to love their husbands and children, to be self-controlled and pure…"

Financial Concerns for Caregivers

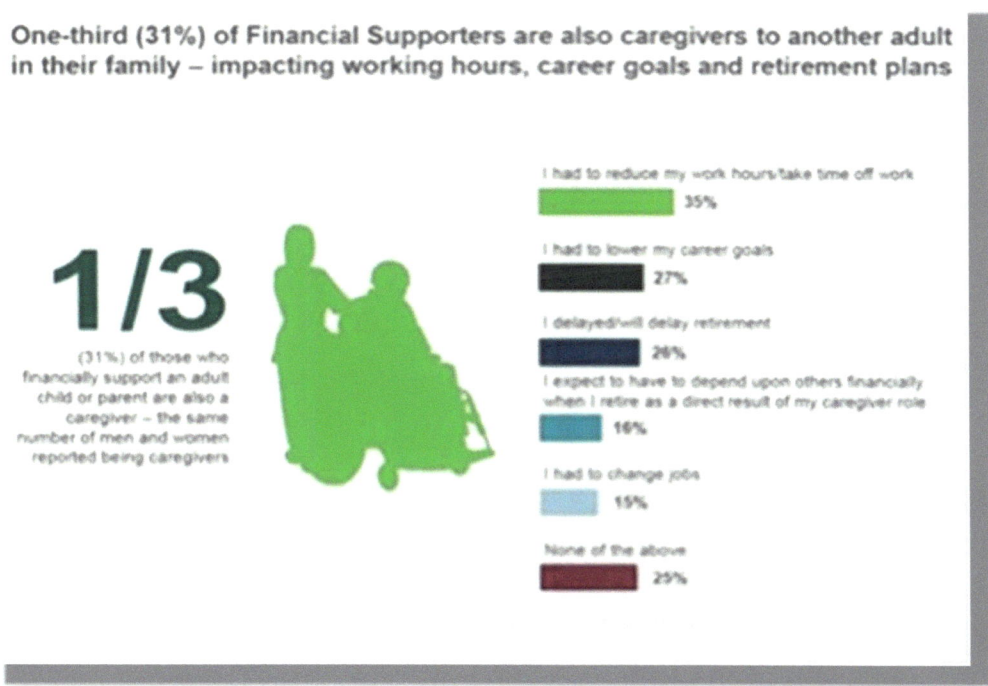

Chapter 16

You'll take care of me when I'm old...right?

Navigational Aids

- What approach can you take to begin talking about elder care?
- What about situations you can't change?
- How stressful is your daily life typically—apart from adding the parent care?
- What are a few ideas to help cope with the stress of elder care?

Chapter 17
Managing and Coping With Stress – Depart on a Smooth Journey
Learning Objectives

After this session you will be able to:

- Identify stressors for each person, and how often they affect them.
- Understand the stressors in their lives.
- Develop effective responses to major or chronic stress.

Introduction

- Stress affects individuals in different ways; there is no universal remedy for stress relief.
- Reducing sources of stress when possible and learning effective methods for coping with stress can both play an important part in dealing with it.

Why is this topic important?

There are two ways to manage stress:
- _____. Some stressors represent things that are controllable (working too many hours). In some cases, it is possible to make choices that actually eliminate the stressor (such as changing jobs).
- _____ When a stressor cannot be removed, look at how you react or control response to the stressor. Learning and using healthy-coping methods can aid your respond to stress in healthier ways.

What Does the Bible Say?

_____, "And why worry about your clothing? Look at the lilies of the field and how they grow. They don't work or make their clothing, yet Solomon in all his glory was not dressed as beautifully as they are. And if God cares so wonderfully for wildflowers that are here today and thrown into the fire tomorrow, he will certainly care for you. Why do you have so little faith?" (NLT)

_____, "Cast all your anxiety on him because he cares for you."

_____, "Come to me, all you who are weary and burdened, and I will give you rest. Take my yoke upon you and learn from me, for I am gentle and humble in heart, and you will find rest for your souls."

Chapter 17

Common Concerns Regarding Stress

Common stressors encountered during a couple's life include:

Stressful Situations and Life Events

- Wedding planning
- Major life changes
- Holidays
- Bereavement
- Chronic or acute health issues

Family stress

- Becoming a parent for the first time
- Caring for an elderly or ill parent or relative
- Intrusive or high-conflict extended family issues
- Last child leaves home ("empty nest")

Relationship Problems

- Marriage breakdowns
- Violence in the home
- Infidelity

Stress at work

- Threat of job loss
- Unrealistic demands

Navigational Aids

Healthy Ways of Dealing with Controllable Stressors

- Identify ways that you can avoid last minute crisis by improving your planning and being more proactive.

- Learn to say "No" more often. Focus on those things that are most important to you and drop the rest.

- When possible, limit the amount of time you spend with people who stress you out.

- Use assertive communication skills more often and also look for opportunities to compromise.

- Ask yourself, "Is the situation really *that* important? Will it matter in five or ten years? In eternity?"

- Can you find anything positive in the situation? If so, choose to focus on that part of the issue more.

- Start an exercise and nutrition program, and get more rest.

Chapter 17

In-Flight Checklist

Use the list on page 44 to identify the important issues you.

1) Choose those that apply within the past 2 years. If the event occurred more than once, mark the number of times beside the score. For example, if you celebrated Christmas each year, mark "2" beside it.

2) For each item on your list, determine which can be changed or resolved and which ones are out of your control. Mark either 'Yes' or 'No' beside each choice.

3) Prioritize the ones you can control and want to work on.

4) Discuss ways you can better cope with the issues that can't be changed or are beyond your control may be experiencing

Download a full copy of Life Events and Stress under Premium Downloads at: http://themarriage-journey.com/premium-resources

Chapter 18
Managing God's Money
Learning Objectives

After this session, you will be able to:

- Confidently discuss the topic of financial management
- Identify common financial pitfalls where couples are vulnerable and work through any financial mismanagement issues.
- Specific steps you can take to manage your finances effectively and in a way that honors the Lord.

Introduction

- It's spoken about in the Bible more often (_____) than heaven.
- Jesus spoke about money more often than about_____ and _____ combined.
- We spend_____ of our waking hours earning, spending or thinking about money.
- Money is one of the most frequently cited causes for _____

"We make a living by what we get, but we make a life by what we give." ~ Winston Churchill

Why is this topic important?

- Money impacts all aspects of our _____ and _____.
- Couples typically resist discussing _____ because they don't want to create problems or start arguments.
- _____ differences eventually leads to _____, anger and failed attempts to address differences.
- _____ Who wait too long to discuss what is bothering them gradually become _____ toward each other.

What Does the Bible Say?

- _____ - "Keep your lives free from the love of money
- and be content with what you have, because God has said, "Never will I leave you; never will I forsake you."
- _____ - "Dishonest money dwindles away, but he who gathers money little by little makes it grow."
- _____ - "The rich rule over the poor, and the borrower is servant to the lender."

Chapter 18

Common Concerns Regarding Finances

Couples tend to need improvement in the following areas:

- Feeling that your_____spending habits are_____than yours.
- _____over the amount of money you should save.
- Concerns about having_____income.
- Not having a specific plan (_____) on how to spend their money or get out of

12 Biblical Principles of Wise Financial Management

1. Everything we have is a_____from Him (Deuteronomy 8:17-18, 1 Corinthians 4:7).
2. The main purpose of_____wealth is to provide for our family (1Timothy 5:8), to help those in need (Proverbs 11:25) and to invest in eternal things (Matthew 6:19-20).
3. _____is God's gift to help us manage our thirst for riches and is the process through which He chooses to bless us (Proverbs 3:10, Malachi 3:10).
4. We should work_____with excellence (Colossians 3:23) and spend less than we earn (Proverbs 21:20).
5. Develop a_____budget.
6. Avoid the use of_____(Proverbs 22:7).
7. Be_____in all financial affairs (Proverbs 3:11, Romans 13:7a, Matthew 22:21b).

8. Be_____with what God provides (Ecclesiastes 5:10, 1Timothy 6:6, Philippians 4:12-13, Hebrews 13:5).

9. Set aside funds for_____. (Proverbs 6:6-8).
10. Be_____, understanding that true generosity always involves_____. (2 Samuel 24:24a, 2 Corinthians 8:1-4, Luke 21:1-4).
11. Get_____counsel from _____ independent financial advisors (Proverbs 11:14, 15:22).
12. Take a day of_____each week (Exodus 23:12a).

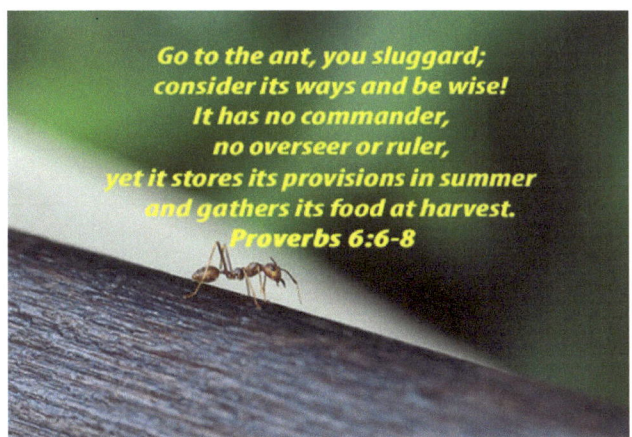

How Would You Handle These Questions?

- "What are some_____short-term and long-term financial_____for us as a couple?"

Chapter 18

- "How can our use of money align better with God's?"
- "How do we determine what _____ to pay off _____?"
- "Now that we know how we each view _____, how should we deal with the _____?"
- "Our finances are tight now. How could we possibly give _____ and _____?"

Principles of Budgeting

- _____ gives you more control over your money, rather than having your bills and spending control your lives.

- Budgeting doesn't just mean _____ _____ on things you really want; rather, it's a way to _____ _____ finances so you can actively decide what to do with your money (e.g. investing, giving).

- Developing a budget can help you out of financial trouble and _____ the associated _____ in your relationship.

Becoming One Financially

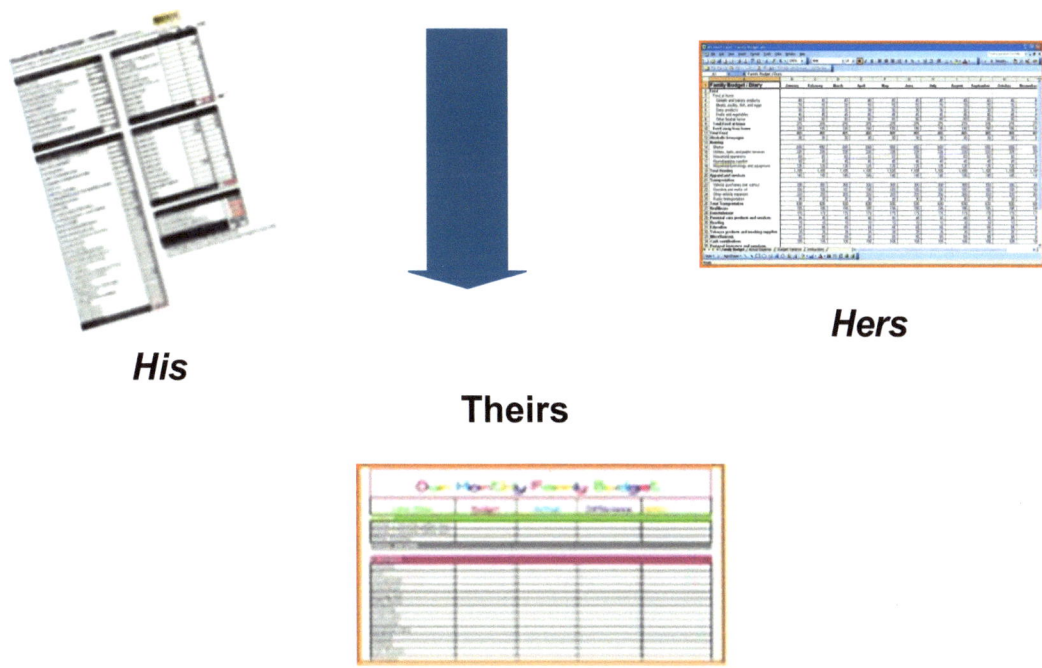

His — *Hers* — *Theirs*

• Debts • Job Security • Long-Term Goals • Credit Cards • Car Replacement • Travel • Wedding Costs

Tips for Merging Finances

1. Discuss and try to understand your money _____.
2. _____, list priorities _____ the top priorities you share and what this means to your budget.
3. Recommend that you get _____ advice. Some conflicts over money come from simply not being aware of options.

Chapter 18

Common Money Traps

- _____ to purchase things that loses value over time (e.g. new car, vacations, furniture) and living beyond your means.
- Buying _____ house, car etc. than you need.
- Credit card debt/only paying the _____ _____ payment.
- Lots of small _____ _____ that add up over time.
- Not giving to _____ work _____.
- Wanting to keep up with your _____ or neighbors.
- Not having a _____ _____ for emergencies.
- Not _____.

Aligning Financial Expectations

Questions for couples to discuss together include:

- Will you have _____ or _____ checking accounts? Who will pay the bills?
- Will you _____ or _____ a home? If renting, how long do you expect to do so?
- How often do you plan on _____ _____? What type of restaurants?
- Will you maintain a _____ budget? Who will maintain it?

Managing God's Money

In-Flight Checklist

1. Are the spending_____considerably different than those of your spouse? What are the most_____factors that influence each of your decisions?

2. Have you both been completely_____about your income, debt, expenses, and financial intentions?

3. Expenditures such as housing, insurances, vehicle maintenance, clothing, medical/dental visits, taxes, food, education and children will affect all marriages at some point. Have you discussed these at _____ and _____?

4. How do you plan to_____discuss your debts and expenses?

5. Have you developed a_____and_____plan in detail? Do you need assistance?

6. Do you have any significant_____about your finances today? What about the future?

Chapter 19
How Cohabitation Impacts the Flight Learning Objectives

After this session, you will be able to:

- Understand the truths about cohabitation.
- Confidently discuss living together before marriage.
- Recognize objective, but nonjudgmental, information in the decision making process about cohabiting.

Introduction

- Cohabitation differs greatly from marriage when it relates to outcomes.
- Cohabiting relationships, even if there is a subsequent marriage, tend to be less enduring.

What Does the Bible Say?

_____, "Marriage should be honored by all, and the marriage bed be kept pure, for God will judge the adulterer and all the sexually immoral."

_____, "Can a man scoop fire into his lap without his clothes being burned?"

_____, "This is why a man leaves his father and mother and bonds with his wife, and they become one flesh."

Common Concerns Regarding Cohabitation

Couples tend to need improvement in the following areas:

- Higher_____or_____rates.
- Adverse_____impact
- Reduced_____.
- Reduced_____quality.
- Increased_____.
- Handling of_____.
- Adverse_____on children.

Chapter 19

The "Myth" Defused

- Cohabiting couples are more likely to experience _____ than married couples.

- Cohabiting men are _____ times as likely as husbands to report _____ in the past year.

- Cohabiting women are _____ times more likely than wives to _____ on their partners.

Adverse Psychological Impact

- Cohabiters report more _____, more _____, and lower levels of _____ and commitment in relationships than married couples.

- Cohabiting _____ have higher rates of _____ than married mothers do.

- 60% of those who had cohabited _____ marriage were more _____ aggressive, _____ supportive of one another, and more _____ than the 40% of spouses who had not lived together.

122

How Cohabitation Impacts the Flight

Couples Over 50 Cohabiting

- _____ Americans aged over 50 were cohabiting by 2010, _____ percent more than in the year 2000 per the Kansas City Star.

    Demographics
    - People who are in their 60s, 70s and 80s now, were in their 20's and 30's in the 1960s and 1970s, which in America were decades of_____ liberalization.

    Personal values
    - Behavioral_____ in society have allowed individual beliefs to manifest.

    Societal norms
    - Trends toward_____ _____ married have made itself evident over the last three decades per research published by Bowling Green State University.

    Economics
    - Among individuals in their fifties, those who are _____ tend to have accumulated _____ wealth than their married peers.

Chapter 19

Cohabitation without Sex

Most couples living together before marriage are sexually involved, what about a cohabiting couple that is not sexually active?

- For example, a couple that lives together for financial reasons but chooses to abstain from sex until marriage?

    o The first issue is_____.
    o Next is the matter of your_____.
    o Thirdly there is the_____of your marriage.
    o When you get married, you are likely to have more_____ with the transition.

Discussion Starters

- How might you living together_____marriage contribute to marital failure?
- Cohabitation as an_____to your marriage.
- Why cohabitation is_____l for your children?
- What are your main_____for and against living together before marriage in_____societies?

How Cohabitation Impacts the Flight

In-Flight Checklist

- How are you dealing with the _____ of living together?
- How has living together impacted your level of lifelong _____ to each other?
- Has your level of _____ in the strength of your relationship _____ since you began cohabiting?

How did you reconcile your _____ teaching and _____ beliefs with your decision to cohabitate?

Chapter 20
Wedding Day Plans - Planning Your Take-off
Learning Objectives

After this session, you will be able to:

- Base your wedding planning decisions on the values and principles that you hold as a couple, not just activities and things.
- Understand the wedding day "is your day."
- Be clear about the expectations you have for each other, and work as a team.

Introduction

- Wedding planning involves two people and two families, which often have different values, expectations, and/or priorities.
- Couples should spend time discussing the values you want to establish in their your together and how you want these values to be reflected in your wedding day plans.
- Wedding planning is burdened with potential conflicts.

Why is this topic important?

- Differences in your family expectations regarding the wedding.
- You, as the bride and groom can be put in the uncomfortable position of mediating between families and friends.
- How do you intend to include cultural and religious differences and how they will be reflected in the wedding ceremony and the reception.

What Does the Bible Say?

- _____, "For this reason, a man will leave his father and mother and be united to his wife, and the two will become one flesh. This is a profound mystery--but I am talking about Christ and the church."

- _____, "Do nothing out of selfish ambition or vain conceit, but in humility consider others better than yourselves. Each of you should look not only to your own interests, but also to the interests of others."

Chapter 20

Common Concerns Regarding Wedding Planning

- What is your wedding_____?
- Your_____ are different than your family and friends.
- Differences in_____ and_____ beliefs.
- Who will you_____, how many?
- Where do you plan to have the_____?

Navigation Aides

- What_____ do you use in determining the decisions to make regarding your wedding and reception?
- What do you want your wedding day to "_____" to others about God?
- What one_____ of your wedding day do you think will be most important to you_____ years later?

128

Wedding Day Plans - Planning Your Take-off

In-Flight Checklist

- Be_____ to those around you.

- Focus on the_____.

- When there is conflict between family expectations, understand that "_____ always talks to_____."

- Prepare_____ _____ and your_____ for the quirks and odd customs of the other family.

- Don't let anyone_____ you with_____ to boycott the wedding or withdraw their support; move ahead and let them make their own decisions.

- Try to keep things in perspective.

Chapter 21
The Holidays - Book Your Travel Plans Early
Learning Objectives

After this session, you will be able to:

- Understand the process of developing holiday plans.
- Identify common celebrations with different expectations you each bring to your relationship.
- Learn specific steps you can take to communicate your holiday desires and plans to friends and family.

Introduction

- Every family has its own attributes for holiday events:
    - Cultural differences
    - Family of origin
    - Tradition
- Lifestyle and Expectations:
    - Emotional expression
    - Spiritual beliefs and values
    - Financial planning
- Together, both families shape your holiday perspective and arrangement.

Chapter 21

Why is this topic important?

- To focus on making pleasant memories for your new family unit.
- To encourage you to take special care of your marriage to overcome the stress before, during and after holidays.
- So that your holidays and traditions can be enjoyed, not become personal prison.

May your roots go down into the soil of God's marvelous LOVE and my you have the power to understand, as all God's people should, how wide, how long, how high, and how deep His love really is.
Ephesians 3:17-18

What Does the Bible Say?

_____, "Therefore do not let anyone judge you by what you eat or drink, or with regard to a religious festival, a New Moon celebration or a Sabbath day. These are a shadow of the things that were to come; the reality, however, is found in Christ."

_____, "Do not let any unwholesome talk come out of your mouths, but only what is helpful for building others up according to their needs, that it may benefit those who listen.."

The Holidays - Book Your Travel Plans Early

Tips on Holiday Planning

- Allow plenty of time for advance planning and discussion.
- Work toward a process that minimizes or eliminates holiday stress.
- Discuss realistic expectations.
- Create a holiday budget using the book's worksheet

Outsider's Unhealthy Expectations

Some dangers that might lead to excessive pressure, manipulation or hostility:

- Share thoughts, suggestions or implications that tend to present feelings of guilt, especially from your family.
- Talk about family customs or traditions you prefer not to use in your relationship, but may feel pressured to follow.
- Explore suggestions how you will share your desires with family and friends?

Chapter 21

How to Share Holiday Plans

- Inform your family and friends well in advance about your plans.
- Explain where and with whom you will spend their holidays.
- Clarify how you can be agreeable and also decisive.
- Be sure you understand celebrations can change.

How to Deal with In-Laws

- How do you plan to begin a conversation with your in-laws?
  - Tip: *The son or daughter is the **icebreaker**.*
- Choose a suitable gift(s) for the recipient(s).
- Accept and show love toward your in-laws?
  - Tip: *Respect and accept the small things*.

The Holidays - Book Your Travel Plans Early

Shared Custody Planning

List the days that may be considered as holidays – for example:

- Basic holidays that usually result in a 3-day weekend, such as President's Day and Columbus Day.

- Holidays that include lengthy time off from school - generally Thanksgiving and Christmas/winter break.

- Consider religious and school holidays.

List Priorities and Conflicts

Holiday Planning Matrix					
Holiday	His Priority (1=Top, 2=Next, etc.)	Her Priority (1=Top, 2=Next, etc.)	Possible Family Conflicts? Who?	Year 1 Holiday Plan	Year 2 Holiday Plan
1)					
2)					
3)					
4)					
5)					
6)					

Source: Adapted from The Solution for Marriages

Chapter 21

Navigation Aides

- How important are holiday celebrations to you and to each of your families?

- What holidays does one family celebrate that the other doesn't?

- How important are the holidays to one spouse that are new or different to the other?

- Are there any holidays that one partner celebrates that the other is opposed to participating in?

"…those who marry will face many troubles in this life…"
(1 Corinthians 7:28)

The Holidays - Book Your Travel Plans Early

In-Flight Checklist

Surviving The Holidays:

- In one sentence share the most significant lesson you take away from this session.

- What personal experience on this topic has been most significant in your life? How did you use it for growth in your relationship?

About the Authors

Mae and Chuck met in 7th grade, dated in High School, and married in 1969, just prior to Chuck's Vietnam tour.

They began mentoring in home Bible studies and saw how their Christ-centered relationship was "different" from others. Though far from "perfect," their marriage and commitment to Christ demonstrated a peace and happiness that intrigued other couples. This became the opportunity to mentor other couples and to teach them to *work* at their relationship and *grow* their *love* for one another (with Christ) each day.

Chuck and Mae have two adult children, Glynn and Barbara, and six grandchildren.

Executive Director and Founder of Today's Promise, Inc., Chuck is an ordained minister with more than 25-years in couple and professional life-coaching experience. Chuck is known as a premier marriage, relationship, budget and career coaching mentor throughout the nation—having been recognized by the NY Times, CBS Evening News, and the Harvard School of Business, among others. Chuck holds a Bachelor of Science in Business and Finance from Barry University, graduating cum laude. He was formerly employed by the Under Secretary of the Treasury in local banks as a loan officer, Junior Vice President, and auditor, which provided unprecedented exposure to the financial industry.

He holds many certifications, including a former Florida State Teaching Certificate as an Occupational Therapist for Secondary Education and a Certified Crown Financial Budget Coach/Counselor. He is a Certified Marriage Mentor a for PREPARE/ENRICH marriage preparation, and he coaches those already married. He holds certification as a Seminar Director for PREPARE/ENRICH, providing training to clergy, professional counselors, and mentor couples. He proudly serves as a 15th Judicial Circuit Court Registered Provider for marriage education, qualifying couples for discounted marriage licensure. Chuck and Mae are certified SYMBIS Facilitators, a premarital training course that teaches specific skills to seriously dating or engaged couples.

Mae retired after serving over 40 years in the local school system. She volunteers at Christ Fellowship Church.

Herman and Sharron Baily recently invited Chuck and Mae as guests on Christian Television Network's *The Herman and Sharon Show* broadcast across 22 stations nation-wide and around the World.
Chuck co-authored *The Solution for Marriages;* dedicated tips to marriage mentors proven to be successful in helping others build the foundation for life- long, satisfying marriages. *The Solution for Marriages* is in English and German.

Their second book, *The Marriage Journey, A Flight Plan to Your Healthy Marriage,* provides the flight plan for marriages to rely on, not if, but when they face the turbulence experienced by every couple. It contains powerful, faith- based references used by the authors in their own 47 plus years of marriage. *The Marriage Journey: A Flight Plan for Your Healthy Marriage* is available in English and Spanish.

Their daily devotional, *Journey 2 Victory: A Devotional Journal* serves as a tool to assist in healing not only marriages and relationships, but also individuals. Many times when thoughts are committed to paper God gives us comfort and 'releases' our hurt and pain. *Journey 2 Victory: A Devotional Journal* is published in English and Spanish.

Their latest publication, *Reignite and Reinvent Your Marriage*, is a seminar workbook designed to provide faith-based skills and habits that will build and strengthen marriages. *Reignite and Reinvent* seminars provide a safe place for couples to reconnect; whether they rate their relationship as a 1 or 10, or anywhere in between. The principles shared in this companion are '*a process*' and not magical.